Dearest Abi

We hope you have the best junior year.
Here's some yummy ideas.

Love you so much,
Mom & Dad
XOXO XO XO XO XOXO

LOVE & LEMONS
EVERY DAY

LOVE & LEMONS
EVERY DAY

More than 100 bright, plant-forward
recipes for every meal

JEANINE DONOFRIO

AVERY

AN IMPRINT OF PENGUIN RANDOM HOUSE

NEW YORK

AVERY

an imprint of Penguin Random House LLC
penguinrandomhouse.com

Most Avery books are available at special quantity discounts for bulk purchase for sales
promotions, premiums, fund-raising, and educational needs. Special books or book excerpts also
can be created to fit specific needs. For details, write SpecialMarkets@penguinrandomhouse.com.

Library of Congress Cataloging-in-Publication Data

Names: Donofrio, Jeanine, author.
Title: Love and lemons every day : more than 100 bright, plant-forward recipes for every meal /
    Jeanine Donofrio.
Description: New York : Avery, an imprint of Penguin Random House, [2019] | Includes index.
Identifiers: LCCN 2018049917| ISBN 9781583335864 (hardcover) | ISBN 9780698404779 (ebook)
Subjects: LCSH: Vegetarian cooking. | Cooking (Natural foods) | LCGFT: Cookbooks.
Classification: LCC TX837 .D63 2019 | DDC 641.5/636—dc23 LC record available at
    https://lccn.loc.gov/2018049917

Printed in China
10 9 8 7 6 5 4 3 2 1

Book design by Trina Bentley of Make & Matter
Food styling by Jeanine Donofrio
Prop styling by Jenn Elliott Blake

To our Love & Lemons blog readers . . .

CONTENTS

LOVE & LEMONS,

The real love story

In 2011, my husband, Jack, and I started a food blog. Back then, that was considered an odd thing given that most people didn't know what a blog was. Our friends wondered why we had camera equipment all over the kitchen, my family wondered why I had largely quit my day job to follow this crazy cooking passion, and our dogs were thrilled that more food than ever before was falling on the floor. I think my dad summed up our new hobby best—"some people pray before they eat their dinner, you guys take pictures of it."

In our first cookbook, I told the story of "Why Love & Lemons," which involved a long blissful walk in Capri and a dog passing us with a lemon in its mouth. It was about a moment in time, just after we had gotten engaged, when we were first inspired to cook with the freshest available locally grown produce. But as all good love stories go, there's also the other side—the part where we were lost and sunburnt by the end of that idyllic Italian hike, where cooking in the kitchen is just plain messy, and when trying to take pictures of it all (with your spouse!) sometimes ends in a giant argument.

During the week we launched our blog, a tray full of naan almost burned our house down, our shiny new camera took a tumble, and food was wilting on the plate before we could manage to get the final shot. These days our process is a bit more streamlined, and if we've learned anything from spending countless hours in the kitchen with each other, it's how to actually work well together. I've stopped getting mad when Jack spills flour all over the floor because his homemade focaccia is so delicious, and Jack is happy to jump on my healthy cooking bandwagon because I regularly use the things he loves like mushrooms, mustard, and anything pickled. He also no longer complains about pitching in and cleaning up . . . especially when "cleaning up" means eating the poached eggs that still taste perfect but aren't photo perfect.

LOVE & LEMONS
EVERY DAY

Jack and I love to walk through farmers markets. He loves to eat cheese samples from the local vendors, and I love to "plan" my meals by scoping out what gorgeous, unique vegetables are awaiting me that day. When we lived in Austin, we did this every weekend, year-round. Now that we've relocated to Chicago, our sunny Sunday market strolls are more seasonally limited.

Our first cookbook was based on those market visits, which is why it's organized by vegetable from A to Z. It's meant to inspire meal ideas depending on what seasonal vegetable you just brought home. That's my favorite way to cook when the markets are overflowing. But when the ground is covered in three feet of snow, we still have to eat. And we still want to eat something delicious and nutritious. (Most likely the Cozy Vegan Mushroom & White Bean Pot Pie on page 141 or the Greek Yogurt Saag Paneer on page 185).

This book is packed with a number of season-specific recipes for your farmers market finds as well as recipes using vegetables and fruits that you can find at pretty much any well-stocked regular grocery store. Of course, I encourage you to seek out local produce whenever possible and to always wait until summer to eat a peach—but know that each and every recipe here was made with things I found near my new home here in the Midwest.

EVERYDAY COOKING,
A LITTLE BIT ELEVATED

During a busy week, my daily meals start to look like this: a green smoothie for breakfast, avocado toast for lunch, and takeout pho for dinner. While that's all well and good, I truly believe that variety is the spice of life and that it *is* possible to fall into too much of a routine (I'm looking at you, oatmeal that I ate every day during college and then not again until ten years later). It's why you won't find a recipe for avocado toast among these pages—I want to bring you new things that you may not have thought of.

What you *will* find are 100+ all-new plant-forward recipes that we love eating in a healthy rotation. Recipes that I've served to eager-to-eat family and friends for years. Some are super quick and perfect for busy mornings and weeknights. Many are great for packing lunches to take to work. Others are meant for nights when you have time to enjoy a well-deserved glass of wine while making dinner.

None of the recipes are complicated to make, and most recipes come with a helpful everyday tip, like how a particular recipe can be made quicker (frozen quinoa!), which recipes are especially great to freeze (most soups!), which salads make great next-day desk lunches (the peach and pole bean salad, page 115, and soba salad, page 117, are two of my favorites!), or if the leftovers from one recipe can be reused for another.

THIS IS THE EXCITING ERA OF THE VEGETABLE!

PLANTS AT THE CENTER OF THE PLATE

You may have noticed a cultural shift in recent years where meat no longer needs to be the star of the plate. There's also been a change in what it means to eat vegetarian, in that meat does not need to be replaced with fake-meat substitutes. This is the exciting era of the vegetable!

SO HOW DO I PUT VEGETABLES AT THE CENTER OF MY PLATE?

I turn to heavy veggie hitters like sweet potatoes, cauliflower, squash, and mushrooms to make meals hearty and filling. I keep a lot of leafy greens on hand because they make me feel energized and light on my feet. I love to use overlooked vegetables like carrots, fennel, beets, rutabaga, and parsnips because I think these humble roots are the cornerstone of cold-season cooking and deserve some creative love too. Of course, when the summer markets are in full force, I stuff my bags full of tomatoes, eggplant, summer squash, peppers, sweet corn, cherries, and my beloved peaches.

LEARNING TO LOVE VEGETABLES

When someone tells me they despise a certain vegetable, my response is always "But you just haven't had it prepared the right way!" My husband, Jack, "hated" asparagus, but once we started grilling thin, snappy spears, he became a believer. For years, I wouldn't touch a cooked carrot until I started roasting them to perfection with robust seasonings. Now I'm crazy for carrots, and you will be too once you try the Moroccan-spiced carrot salad on page 121.

This is not a book about becoming vegetarian, it's a book about loving vegetables because they're versatile and fun to cook. Butternut squash becomes a creamy queso dip that your guests will devour at your next gathering (page 75), a whole stalk of broccoli becomes a spicy "rice" burrito filling (page 149), and a rutabaga transforms into a hearty meatless ragu (page 189).

We've all pushed aside mushy, under-seasoned vegetables, but I'm here to say—give peas a chance! Just don't overcook them.

FLAVOR IN VEGETARIAN COOKING

It took me a while to love my veggies. I recall sitting across the dinner table from my little sister, us making faces at each other for an hour while we tried to finish our cold broccoli. Years later, I surprised everyone—myself included—when I decided to become vegetarian, especially because the only dishes I knew how to "cook" were bland stir-fries and microwaved frozen vegetables. As I was losing patience with my flavorless new lifestyle, the most glorious thing happened—I discovered my first falafel. The bold spices, punchy herbs, and lemony hummus stuffed into that pita made me realize that vegetables could be exciting! There were so many new-to-me flavors to try! So what do I know now that I wish I knew back then? That making vegetables insanely delicious requires a balance of these elements.

LEMONS (OF COURSE!), OR LIMES OR VINEGARS, FOR POP

This probably goes without saying, but I love lemons to brighten up any dish. What I mean by "brighten" is that lemons, as well as other acids, work in contrast to salt and fats to create a full, well-rounded flavor. If you ever feel that something tastes a little flat, try adding a squeeze of lemon, lime, or a drizzle of vinegar to liven things up.

SALT & SALTY THINGS

Salt gets a bad rap, because a lot of American prepackaged and fast foods contain too much sodium. But when you're cooking from scratch with mostly raw vegetables, they need plenty of salt. Salt is the ultimate flavor enhancer—it makes things taste like the best versions of themselves. For example, if you sprinkle salt on a tomato, it doesn't make the tomato taste like salt, it brings out its inherent sweetness. The recipes in this book call for fine-grain sea salt, which has the same texture as regular table salt without the bitter taste of iodized salt. Occasionally, I'll use flaky sea salt like Maldon as a finishing salt. When I don't use salt, I incorporate other salty ingredients like miso paste or tamari.

HEALTHY FATS

Healthy fat is vitally important in plant-forward food because it's what makes you feel full and satiated at the end of a meal. Not only do salads dressed with olive oil, sandwiches with avocado, and brownies made with coconut oil taste better than their fat-free equivalents, but they also make me feel like I need to eat less of them to feel satisfied. So don't be afraid of healthy fats—they're what make you happy to eat only one brownie instead of the entire pan!

LOTS & LOTS OF HERBS & SPICES

Flavoring with herbs and spices is like putting paint to canvas. You can decide whether you like cerulean blue versus ultramarine just like you can decide if you prefer basil over cilantro. If you're like me, you love both basil and cilantro, and also fresh parsley, thyme, rosemary, and mint, depending on the season or even your mood. I use thyme when I'm craving something cozy, rosemary to warm up a winter day, and basil or mint when I'm celebrating the sun of spring or summer.

The same goes for spices. Remember my glorious first falafel? I loved it so much because it packed a punch with spices I continue to use—cumin, coriander, and cayenne. Of course, there are a ton of other spices to choose from: smoked paprika has an almost bacon-like flavor, cinnamon adds a warm homey-ness even in savory dishes (see tagine, page 207), caraway seeds make harissa rich and zippy (page 281), and curry spices like turmeric and cardamom add richness that fats, acids, and salts cannot add on their own.

WHEN PLANTS ARE AT THE CENTER OF THE PLATE— CHOOSE GOOD ONES!

If you're like us, living in a cold climate, you may not be able to get to a farmers market during the middle of winter. The vast majority of the recipes in this book will work with decent-looking produce from your grocery store. But when spring rolls around—get out there, get some fresh air, and explore your local markets! Why should you care about choosing produce that's local and in season? The shortest answer is—it tastes best! Plants that have traveled less have been harvested closer to their ideal time of ripeness. This means that local, in-season tomatoes are sweeter and juicier than their distant counterparts, kale is softer and more delicate, arugula is wonderfully spicy, carrots are sweeter and snappier, leeks are melt-in-your-mouth tender and sweet, and juicy berries are bursty instead of bland. If you're not sure what's in season when, here's a simple guide.

SEASONAL PRODUCE GUIDE

SPRING	SUMMER	FALL	WINTER
Asparagus	Berries	Apples	Beets
Avocados	Cantaloupe	Beets	Brussels Sprouts
Broccoli	Carrots	Broccoli	Cabbage
Carrots	Cherries	Brussels Sprouts	Carrots
Collard Greens	Collard Greens	Cabbage	Fennel
Kale	Corn	Carrots	Grapefruit
Leeks	Cucumber	Cauliflower	Kale
Lettuce	Eggplant	Collard Greens	Leeks
Mangoes	Green Beans	Grapes	Lemons
Mushrooms	Melon	Green Beans	Onions
Onions	Okra	Kale	Oranges
Peas	Peaches	Mushrooms	Parsnips
Radishes	Peppers	Parsnips	Pears
Ramps	Plums	Pears	Potatoes
Rhubarb	Raspberries	Potatoes	Pumpkins
Spinach	Tomatillos	Pumpkins	Rutabagas
Strawberries	Tomatoes	Radishes	Sweet Potatoes
Swiss Chard	Yellow Squash	Sweet Potatoes	Turnips
Turnips	Zucchini	Winter Squash	Winter Squash

Availability of produce varies by region and climate.

WAIT—WHAT ABOUT PROTEIN?

Protein is an important part of a well-balanced dish, but if vegetables are at the center of the plate, where does that put protein? Well, supporting the vegetables of course. While protein needs vary from person to person, here are some of my favorite non-meat proteins that you'll see throughout the recipes in this book.

PLANT-BASED PROTEINS

CHICKPEAS

Funny story—I love chickpeas so much that I almost named the blog "Chickpea Chick." I'm glad I didn't, because I'm not sure Jack would have wanted to be "Mr. Chickpea Chick." Naming aside, they're so versatile and easy to keep on hand for soups, stews, salads, curries, or any meal that needs to be bulked up.

BLACK BEANS & CANNELLINI BEANS

Of course there are more types of beans, but these two are readily available, and I use them all the time. If you want to think outside the bean box, you could play around with subbing adzuki or pinto beans for black beans, or navy beans for cannellini.

LENTILS

I'll be honest—aside from lentil soup, it took me a while to love lentils. The problem is that they can easily become mushy and bland. I finally discovered that the key is to take advantage of the texture. Red lentils are wonderful for thickening stews and holding together falafel (page 137). French lentils, when cooked al dente, are wonderful in salads. To contrast their earthy flavor, I like to brighten them up with plenty of lemon juice and vinegars.

NUTS

Nuts are great for snacking and adding crunch to a dish. But they're especially magical when blended into creamy non-dairy sauces. Cashews become a luscious pasta sauce, and walnuts make a hearty miso sauce for the buddha bowls on page 147. And don't forget about nut butters, which I love not only as a snack, but as a binder and to provide richness in vegan baked goods like cookies and brownies.

Produce has protein too! Some of my favorite vegetables, including peas, spinach, kale, broccoli, Brussels sprouts, and avocados, all have protein!

TOFU

It has such a bad reputation for being bland, but that's because it *is* bland—spice it up! It's only as good as what you put on it. Don't miss the tofu scramble on page 43—we love it as much as we love our egg scrambles.

QUINOA

Quinoa is the "queen" of grains because it's packed with 14 grams of protein per serving. It's also one of the most versatile ingredients—grain or protein—that I use. I love it not only in soups, salads, and bowls—it also works incorporated into a stuffing for vegetables like acorn squash. You can even use it in baking and dessert! Flip to page 35 and go make the Banana Bread Quinoa Breakfast Cookies. Is there anything quinoa can't do?

SEEDS

When I take a break from topping things with toasted nuts, I'll use toasted sunflower seeds, hemp seeds, sesame seeds, chia seeds, or pepitas. Seeds, like nuts, are concentrated sources of protein and fat. Hemp seeds provide a quick sprinkle of protein, sesame seeds add nutty richness (the sesame crackers on page 77 are my favorite snack), pepitas make the most vibrant green pestos, flaxseeds are necessary to bind vegan baked goods, and chia seeds make a delicious pudding (page 257).

VEGETARIAN PROTEINS

EGGS

Want an easy way to bump up the protein in just about anything? Put a poached egg on it. I recommend buying organic, cage-free eggs, locally sourced if possible.

DAIRY

My favorite source of dairy protein is Greek yogurt. It's easier to digest than most other forms of dairy, and I feel great eating it. As for cheese, a sprinkle of feta cheese is my go-to topping—its pop of flavor goes a long way.

GRAINS

Start by rinsing the grains. Place the dry grains in a strainer that fits inside of a bowl and rinse a few times until the water in the bowl is clear. Drain and you're ready to cook.

Buckwheat	1 cup dry + 2 cups water Yield: 3 cups cooked	Bring to a boil. Reduce the heat and simmer, uncovered, for 10 minutes, or until tender. Drain and rinse with cold water until the water runs clear.
Farro or wheat berries	1 cup dry + pot of water Yield: 3 cups cooked	Bring to a boil. Reduce the heat and simmer, uncovered, 25 to 40 minutes for farro and soft wheat berries, 45 to 60 minutes for hard wheat berries, or until tender. Add more water if necessary. Drain excess water.
Bulgur	1 cup dry + 2 cups water Yield: 2½ cups cooked	Bring the water to a boil and stir in the bulgur. Cover, turn off the heat, and set aside for 20 to 30 minutes, or until tender. Drain excess water. Fluff with a fork.
Quinoa	1 cup dry + 1¾ cups water Yield: 3 cups cooked	Bring to a boil. Cover, reduce the heat, and simmer for 15 minutes. Remove from the heat and let sit, covered, for 10 minutes. Fluff with a fork.
Short-grain brown rice	1 cup dry + 2 cups water + 1 teaspoon extra-virgin olive oil Yield: 3 cups cooked	Bring to a boil. Cover, reduce the heat, and simmer for 45 minutes. Remove from the heat and let sit, covered, for 10 minutes. Fluff with a fork.
White jasmine or basmati rice	1 cup dry + 1½ cups water + 1 teaspoon extra-virgin olive oil Yield: 3 cups cooked	Bring to a boil. Cover, reduce the heat, and simmer for 15 minutes. Remove from the heat and let sit, covered, for 10 minutes. Fluff with a fork.

LEGUMES

{ BEAN PREP }

Place the beans in a large bowl. Discard any stones or debris.
Cover with 2 to 3 inches of water and discard any beans that float.
Soak at room temperature for 8 hours or overnight. Drain and rinse well.

Black beans	1 cup dry + pot of water Yield: 3 cups cooked	Place in a pot and cover with at least 2 inches of water. Bring to a boil. Reduce the heat and simmer, uncovered, stirring occasionally, for 45 minutes to 1 hour, or until tender.
Cannellini beans	1 cup dry + pot of water Yield: 3 cups cooked	Place in a pot and cover with at least 2 inches of water. Bring to a boil. Reduce the heat and simmer, uncovered, stirring occasionally, for 1½ to 2 hours, or until tender.
Chickpeas	1 cup dry + pot of water Yield: 3 cups cooked	Place in a pot and cover with at least 2 inches of water. Bring to a boil. Reduce the heat and simmer, uncovered, stirring occasionally, for 1½ to 2 hours, or until tender.

{ LENTIL PREP }

Rinse, drain, and continue with cooking instructions. No need to soak. Alternatively,
add dry lentils directly to soups and stews and cook until tender and thickened.

French green lentils	1 cup dry + 3 cups water Yield: 3 cups cooked	Bring to a boil. Cover, reduce the heat, and simmer, stirring occasionally, for 20 to 30 minutes, or until tender.
Red and yellow lentils	1 cup dry + 1½ cups water Yield: 3 cups cooked	Bring to a boil. Cover, reduce the heat, and simmer, stirring occasionally, for 10 to 15 minutes, or until tender.

Don't toss those tops ...
or those stems, ends, nubs,
or greens either.

WASTE NOT,

Here are my favorite ways to use "scrap parts" that are commonly thrown out:

BEET GREENS

1 | Finely chop and make gremolata (see Beet Salad with Pistachio Beet Green Gremolata, page 127).

2 | Sauté them as you would chard or kale—in a little olive oil with minced garlic and a squeeze of lemon. Enjoy as a side dish or toss them into pasta with feta cheese, olive oil, and (more) lemon!

CARROT TOPS

1 | Use in sauces, like Carrot Top Tzatziki with roasted carrots on page 229.

2 | Blend into pesto (page 304).

3 | Chop into chimichurri (replace half the herbs with carrot tops in the recipe on page 283).

WANT NOT

BROCCOLI STALKS

1 | Use in most recipes that call for broccoli (stir-fries, pastas, stews, etc.). Just chop up the stems into finer pieces so that they become tender when cooked.

2 | Puree the whole head of broccoli into soup (see Creamy Broccoli Soup in *The Love & Lemons Cookbook*).

3 | Thinly shave or spiralize the stalk into salads.

4 | Pulse in a food processor to make broccoli "rice" (see Broccoli Rice Black Bean Burritos, page 149).

CAULIFLOWER CORES

1 | Roast the whole cauliflower, cores and all (see Turmeric-Spiced Whole Roasted Cauliflower, page 187).

2 | Make cauliflower steaks with slabs cut from the whole cauliflower (see Cauliflower Steaks with Lemon Salsa Verde, page 145).

3 | Roast or blanch leftover cores and use as a thickener in blended soups.

CILANTRO STEMS

Finely chop the stems and include in any recipe that calls for cilantro. Note that the stems have more flavor than the leaves, so I love to use them to add bold flavor to soups (see Coconut Soup with Sweet Potato & Kale, page 85) and rice (see Broccoli Rice Black Bean Burritos, page 149).

CORN COBS

1 | "Milk" the corn cobs. Once the kernels have been sliced off, use the back of a chef's knife to scrape the milky liquid that's left on the cob. Include it in saucy corn recipes such as soups and pastas (see Creamy Sweet Corn Pappardelle, page 167).

2 | Use the leftover cobs in your summer vegetable broth (see Scrap Stock, page 106).

KALE STEMS

1 | Finely chop the stems and use them in any recipe where you're sautéeing the kale. Add the stems earlier in the cooking process so that they become tender.

2 | Blanch and mix into pesto (replace carrot tops with blanched kale stems in the recipe on page 304).

3 | A funny thing—our dogs love to eat chopped up kale stems; maybe yours will, too!

RADISH GREENS

1 | Sauté them in olive oil with garlic, salt, and pepper and finish with a squeeze of lemon.

2 | Make the Leek & Radish Green Tart on page 181 that uses both the greens and the radishes.

3 | Fold the sautéed radish greens into omelets. They taste great with eggs, and their bitter flavor becomes more mellow.

4 | Blanch and blend them into the Radish-Green Goddess sauce on page 221.

SCRAPS BEST FOR STOCK: CARROT TOPS, ONION ENDS, CELERY LEAVES, FENNEL FRONDS, LEEK TOPS, SCALLION TOPS.

Store these bits in a bag in the freezer until you have enough to make stock! (See page 106.)

MY FAVORITE THINGS

High-speed blender

I love my Vitamix® blender. When I first got it, I had no idea that it would be a game-changing kitchen appliance. I use it nearly every day to make the creamiest smoothies, the smoothest nondairy sauces, and the most velvety soups. It's especially useful to make my Creamy Sweet Corn Pappardelle (page 167), the healthier "Hollandaise" sauce for my Caprese Eggs Benedict with Healthier Hollandaise (page 41), and the curry sauce for my Sunshine Sweet Potato Curry (page 193).

A good chef's knife

You don't have to have the most expensive knife on the block, just a sharp, good-quality one. Your knife should be proportionate to the size of your hand. As a short person with small hands, I use a knife that is much smaller than the fancy chef's knives you see on TV.

Good cutting board

A good wooden cutting board will save your knives. Over the years, I've tried many different types, and my large maple Boos® board has held up the best. I like to use an oversize cutting board so that I can chop and prep lots of vegetables at once!

Cast-iron pans

I use a cast-iron pan when I want a really good sear on my food. Because a cast-iron pan gets so hot, mushrooms get nicely browned around the edges, and Brussels sprouts get a deep char. I love mine for frittatas because the pan can go straight from the stovetop to the oven. It's also necessary to get crisp-edged socca in my Spring-on-a-Plate Socca Flatbread (page 153). I use a 12-inch Staub® fry pan, and I also love their large cocottes for soups and stews.

Cast-iron grill pan

I love to grill outside in the summertime, but when summer's over, it's so much easier to cook indoors on a cast-iron grill pan. I use mine to get a nice char on the mushrooms in my Vegetarian Portobello Reuben Sandwiches (page 169), and my Rainbow Summer Veggie Skewers (page 163) come out great on the grill pan too.

Nonstick skillet

A nonstick skillet is especially useful for cooking eggs and pancakes. GreenPan® is my favorite brand because its ceramic surface doesn't chip off, making it a safe, nontoxic alternative to older nonstick pans.

Microplane zester

There's a lot of lemon zest in this book, so get your zester ready!

Mandoline

Aside from the way a vegetable is cooked, the *cut* of the vegetable can entirely transform it. For example, you might not enjoy large chunks of raw radish, but when they're sliced paper-thin, the crisp texture is delightful. The mandoline is especially useful to cut paper-thin fennel for the Sesame-Ginger Avocado Fennel Salad (page 113) and to thinly slice cabbage for the Tahini Collard Green Slaw (page 225).

Food processor, medium and small

A large, bulky food processor drives me crazy . . . so the recipes in this book that call for a food processor (for example, the Baked Red Lentil Falafel, page 137, and the Chickpea Harissa Veggie Burgers, page 173) can be made in a medium 7-cup KitchenAid® food processor. For smaller-batch pestos, sauces, and salsas, I prefer to use a 3- to 4-cup food processor.

EVERYDAY
TIPS

Set up a mise en place. This sounds fancy, but it just means prepping and chopping all your ingredients, then setting them out before starting to cook. By taking a little time to get organized, the cooking process goes more quickly and easily—you won't have onions burning while you're still chopping celery.

Spoon and level. For baked goods, spoon the flour into a measuring cup, then level it with a knife. This ensures that your flour measurement will be accurate—too much flour will make your baked goods dense and/or dry.

Batch cook and freeze. Lentils and grains freeze so well! The more you can cook and freeze at once, the shorter your future cook times will be. See page 38 for my method for freezing grains.

Spice to your own level. Depending on the climate and season in which they're grown, peppers like jalapeños and serranos vary tremendously in spice level. Depending on freshness, even dried spices like chili powder and red pepper flakes have quite a range. If you're sensitive to spice, start with less. If you love things spicy—add more!

Taste and adjust. Vegetables can vary in size, freshness, water content, and flavor. For instance, a carrot you get from the farmers market may have a more concentrated flavor than a grocery store carrot. Because every vegetable is different, it's best to always taste a dish before serving it and adjust final seasonings according to your liking. Often, an extra pinch of salt and a little pepper make all the difference in bumping up flavor.

QUICK FLAVOR FIXES

Bland?
Add salt, pepper, and possibly more acid like another squeeze of lemon, lime, or vinegar (whichever is in the recipe) to help flavors pop.

Still bland?
Try adding more of the seasonings that are in the recipe (cumin, coriander, etc.), since dry spices can vary widely in potency.

Too tangy?
Add a drizzle of olive oil or some sweetness like a pinch of sugar, a drizzle of maple syrup, or a drop of honey.

Too spicy?
Add a few drops of white wine vinegar or rice vinegar to tone it down.

Still too spicy?
Add more of whatever fat is in the recipe (e.g., olive oil), and try adding some sweetness.

Not spicy enough?
Add more red pepper flakes, chile peppers, or sriracha.

BREA

KFAST

BANANA BREAD QUINOA BREAKFAST COOKIES

These cookies are a well-balanced breakfast in cookie form! They're soft, similar to muffin tops, and, thanks to the oats, they're gluten-free. With almond butter and quinoa, they even contain protein. I like to eat one and freeze the rest so that I can have a banana bready breakfast every day!

◆

1 tablespoon ground flaxseed

3 tablespoons water

1 cup Homemade Oat Flour (page 61)

1 cup gluten-free whole rolled oats

½ teaspoon baking powder

½ teaspoon baking soda

½ teaspoon cinnamon

½ teaspoon sea salt

½ cup cooked quinoa (page 22)

¼ cup walnuts, chopped

½ cup almond butter

¼ cup maple syrup

½ cup mashed banana (about 1 medium)

1 teaspoon vanilla extract

2 tablespoons melted coconut oil

Preheat the oven to 350°F and line a large baking sheet with parchment paper.

In a small bowl, combine the ground flaxseed and water and set aside to thicken for about 5 minutes.

In a large bowl, stir together the oat flour, whole oats, baking powder, baking soda, cinnamon, and salt. Fold in the quinoa and walnuts.

In a medium bowl, combine the almond butter, maple syrup, mashed banana, vanilla, coconut oil, and the thickened flaxseed mixture. Whisk until well combined.

Pour the wet ingredients into the bowl of dry ingredients and fold in until just combined.

Use a ¼-cup cookie scoop to scoop the batter onto the baking sheet. Bake for 20 to 22 minutes, or until lightly browned and crisp. Cool on the pan for 5 minutes and then transfer to a wire rack to finish cooling.

When cookies are completely cool, they can be stored in an airtight container.

MAKES 12 LARGE COOKIES

VEGAN & GLUTEN-FREE

TIP I like to freeze quinoa (page 38) so that I always have precooked quinoa on hand. Let it thaw at room temperature for about 30 minutes after removing from the freezer.

VEGAN:

In a small bowl, whisk 2 tablespoons ground flaxseed with 6 tablespoons water. Set aside to thicken for 5 minutes, then add to the wet mixture in place of the eggs. Add an additional 1 teaspoon baking powder to help the pancakes rise.

LEMON CORNMEAL PANCAKES

My obsession with lemony pancakes started way back in college, almost by accident. My roommate and I were reading the back of the pancake box, and it said to add lemon for extra-rich pancakes. The difference was subtle but life changing. It was the first time I realized the power that lemon has to add brightness and dimension to so many types of foods. Maybe that was truly the start of Love & Lemons? Since then I've ditched the boxed mix, and I make these homemade pancakes with cornmeal and whole wheat pastry flour. Since I like my pancakes extra lemony, I squeeze a little lemon on them before pouring on the maple syrup.

❖

1¾ cups whole wheat pastry flour*

½ cup cornmeal

2 tablespoons cane sugar

2 teaspoons baking powder

1 teaspoon baking soda

½ teaspoon sea salt

1½ cups almond milk

1 tablespoon lemon zest

2 tablespoons fresh lemon juice, plus more for squeezing

2 large eggs

¼ cup extra-virgin olive oil, plus more for the pan

For Serving

Maple syrup

Butter (optional)

Fruit of your choice (optional)

Or 1 cup all-purpose flour plus ¾ cup whole wheat flour

In a large bowl, combine the flour, cornmeal, sugar, baking powder, baking soda, and salt.

In a small bowl, whisk together the almond milk, lemon zest, lemon juice, eggs, and olive oil until lightly frothy.

Pour the wet ingredients into the bowl with the dry ingredients and stir until just combined. A few lumps are okay.

Heat a nonstick skillet or griddle to medium heat. Brush the skillet with a little olive oil and use a ⅓-cup scoop to pour the batter. Cook the pancakes until the bottoms are golden brown and the tops are bubbly (the vegan version will not bubble as much), about 2 minutes, turning the heat to low as needed. Flip, and cook for another 2 minutes.

I suggest making one test pancake to figure out the exact time and temperature of your pan, as this varies depending on your stovetop and cookware. Serve pancakes with squeezes of lemon, maple syrup, butter, and fruit, if desired.

MAKES 12 ┆ **SERVES** 4

TIP ┆ These freeze well!

HOW TO FREEZE QUINOA & OTHER GRAINS

I love to have frozen grains on hand to save time when I make my favorite recipes. With quinoa at the ready, I can quickly make my Banana Bread Quinoa Breakfast Cookies (page 35) or Miso Quinoa Bowls with Kale & Eggs (page 45). When I make my Sunshine Sweet Potato Curry (page 193) and Greek Yogurt Saag Paneer (page 185), I simply heat frozen rice for serving. Farro is another great grain to freeze, and it's fantastic tossed into easy herb-flecked side dishes (see Sweet Potato Wedges with Farro & Tahini, page 219).

Freezing grains is simple! Here's how I do it:

1.
Cook the grains according to the directions on page 22 and let cool slightly.

2.
Spread them into a thin layer on a parchment-lined baking sheet.

3.
Place the baking sheet carefully in your freezer. Freeze for at least 2 hours, or until fully frozen.

4.
Remove the sheet from the freezer and transfer the frozen grains to a freezer-safe container.

To thaw: Let sit at room temperature for 30 minutes, or until thawed. Use immediately in cold dishes, or gently reheat to add to warm recipes.

CAPRESE EGGS BENEDICT WITH HEALTHIER HOLLANDAISE

I love caprese salad so much that I decided to make breakfast out of it. Tomatoes, basil, and a poached egg (instead of soft mozzarella) are so yummy atop toasted English muffins. But the real star of this recipe is the sauce. Traditional hollandaise, while delicious, is too rich and fussy for me to make at home. This tangy, creamy cashew sauce is simple to make in the blender, and it can be stored in the fridge for multiple days.

8 tomato slices

Balsamic vinegar, for drizzling

Sea salt and freshly ground black pepper

8 poached eggs (page 60)

4 English muffins, toasted

8 large basil leaves

4 teaspoons chopped chives

Healthier Hollandaise

½ cup raw cashews

¼ cup water

2 tablespoons extra-virgin olive oil

2 teaspoons fresh lemon juice

¼ teaspoon Dijon mustard

½ garlic clove

⅛ teaspoon ground turmeric

¼ teaspoon sea salt

Freshly ground black pepper

Place the sliced tomatoes on a plate, drizzle with balsamic vinegar, and season with salt and pepper. Set aside.

Make the cashew hollandaise: In a high-speed blender, place the cashews, water, olive oil, lemon juice, mustard, garlic, turmeric, salt, and a few grinds of black pepper and process into a smooth sauce. Transfer to a small bowl and set aside. The sauce can be made in advance and stored in the fridge.

Make the poached eggs.

When you're ready to serve, check the sauce, and if necessary, stir in a tiny bit of water so it's a thick but drizzleable consistency.

Assemble each plate with two halves of the toasted English muffins and top each half with a tomato slice, a basil leaf, a poached egg, and a generous drizzle of the sauce. Season with salt and pepper to taste, top with the fresh chives, and serve.

SERVES 4

VEGAN: Use baked smoked tofu instead of the egg.

GLUTEN-FREE: Use gluten-free English muffins or toast.

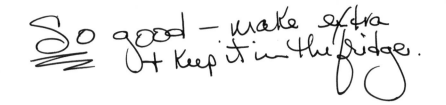

So good — make extra & keep it in the fridge.

YELLOW SQUASH TURMERIC TOFU SCRAMBLE

Before you flip the page because you think you're not a tofu person, you *have* to give this one a try! Tofu acts as a flavor sponge, so it needs a bunch of seasoning to really shine. In this recipe, cumin and turmeric add flavor, Dijon mustard adds a necessary "eggy" taste, and the almond milk–nutritional yeast mixture makes it more like a creamy, soft scramble. The yellow squash and its egg-like color intermingle with the tofu, adding a bit more veggie punch to your breakfast.

½ cup unsweetened almond milk

2 tablespoons nutritional yeast

2 garlic cloves, minced

¼ teaspoon ground turmeric

¼ teaspoon ground cumin

¼ teaspoon Dijon mustard

¼ teaspoon sea salt, plus more to taste

1 tablespoon extra-virgin olive oil

½ cup diced yellow onion

1 small yellow squash, diced

12 ounces extra-firm tofu, water pressed out and crumbled

1 jarred roasted red bell pepper, diced

Freshly ground black pepper

For Serving

1 avocado, sliced

Lemon wedge

Red pepper flakes

8 tortillas, warmed

Microgreens (optional)

In a small bowl, whisk together the almond milk, nutritional yeast, garlic, turmeric, cumin, mustard, and salt. Set aside.

Heat the olive oil in a large skillet over medium heat. Add the onion, squash, and a few generous pinches of salt and pepper and cook until soft, about 5 minutes. Stir in the tofu and red pepper and cook for 3 to 5 minutes, until the tofu is thoroughly heated. Reduce the heat to low and stir in the almond milk mixture. Cook 3 minutes, stirring occasionally, then remove from the heat. Season to taste.

Season the avocado slices with a squeeze of lemon and a pinch of salt and red pepper flakes. Serve alongside the tofu scramble with tortillas and microgreens, if using.

SERVES 4 | VEGAN | GLUTEN-FREE: Use corn tortillas.

TIP | Unlike scrambles made with eggs, this scramble keeps very well in the fridge. Reheat leftovers and make breakfast tacos throughout the week.

MISO QUINOA BOWLS WITH KALE & EGGS

This is inspired by a breakfast bowl I had at a restaurant called Egg Shop in New York. As we sat down with menus, Jack pointed to a bowl whose description listed "quinoa, kale, avocado, and eggs" and said, "I know what you're having." I loved it so much that the second we got home, I came up with this breakfast bowl, loosely inspired by their flavors. It's so simple to make, and the lemon juice, miso paste, and Dijon mustard really pack a punch. You'll love eating kale for breakfast!

◆——◆◆——◆

1 tablespoon white miso paste

3 tablespoons water

1 tablespoon fresh lemon juice

¼ teaspoon Dijon mustard

Extra-virgin olive oil, for drizzling

2 tablespoons finely sliced scallions

5 kale leaves, stems finely diced, leaves chopped (about 3 cups)

1½ cups cooked quinoa (page 22)

Sea salt and freshly ground black pepper

1 tablespoon minced fresh dill

2 soft-boiled eggs (page 60)

1 red radish, thinly sliced

½ avocado, sliced

¼ cup microgreens (optional)

Pinch of red pepper flakes (optional)

In a small bowl, whisk together the miso paste, water, lemon juice, and mustard.

In a large nonstick skillet over medium heat, lightly coat the bottom of the pan with a drizzle of olive oil. Add the scallions, kale stems, and quinoa and cook for 3 minutes, stirring, until the scallions and kale stems are soft and the quinoa is lightly toasted. Add the kale leaves and a pinch of salt and pepper and toss until gently wilted, about 1 minute. Stir in the dill.

Make the soft-boiled eggs. Divide the kale and quinoa mixture between 2 bowls. Drizzle with half of the miso dressing. Top with the soft-boiled eggs, radish, avocado, microgreens, and red pepper flakes, if desired. Drizzle with the remaining dressing.

SERVES 2   VEGAN: Skip the egg.   GLUTEN-FREE

TIP This is a great recipe to use up leftover quinoa that you might have on hand.

STRAWBERRY BAKED FRENCH TOAST

This is the perfect recipe for hosting an easy weekend brunch. A good dash of warming spices—cinnamon, nutmeg, ginger, cardamom—and a touch of black pepper (you won't taste the pepper, I promise!) make this so flavorful. If fresh strawberries are out of season, you can use frozen berries in a pinch.

❖

3 large eggs

¾ cup almond milk

1 tablespoon maple syrup, plus more for serving

1 tablespoon cinnamon

½ teaspoon nutmeg

½ teaspoon ground ginger

¼ teaspoon ground cardamom

⅛ teaspoon sea salt

⅛ teaspoon freshly ground black pepper

10 (1-inch-thick) challah bread slices, cubed (8 cups)

16 ounces strawberries, hulled and halved

⅓ cup sliced almonds

1 teaspoon melted coconut oil, plus more for greasing

Preheat the oven to 400°F and grease an 8 x 11-inch or similar baking dish with coconut oil.

In a large bowl, combine the eggs, almond milk, maple syrup, cinnamon, nutmeg, ginger, cardamom, salt, and pepper. Beat until combined. Add the bread cubes and half of the strawberries and toss to coat. Pour the mixture into the prepared baking dish and top with the remaining strawberries and the almonds. Drizzle the coconut oil on top and bake for 18 minutes, or until the tops of the bread cubes are lightly browned.

Remove from the oven and serve with maple syrup.

SERVES 6

TIP

If your polenta becomes too thick, whisk in more water and/or a few drizzles of olive oil to reach your desired consistency.

BREAKFAST POLENTA BOWLS WITH CHIMICHURRI

Everyone is crazy for overnight oats, but here's my version of "overnight polenta." With two easy prep steps, you'll save at least 40 minutes of cooking (and stirring) time when you're ready to make the polenta. This is a great recipe to use up leftover roasted vegetables and sauces (i.e., chimichurri and harissa) that you might have on hand.

---

1 cup stone-ground polenta

1 cup water

1 bunch broccolini, chopped into 1-inch pieces, including stems

1 small sweet potato, cubed

1 parsnip, chopped into ½-inch pieces

Extra-virgin olive oil, for drizzling

2 cups unsweetened almond milk

½ teaspoon sea salt, plus more for sprinkling

Freshly ground black pepper

Homemade Harissa (page 281), or store-bought (optional)

½ cup microgreens (optional)

Chimichurri

⅓ cup extra-virgin olive oil

3 tablespoons white wine vinegar

1 garlic clove, minced

½ teaspoon red pepper flakes

¼ teaspoon smoked paprika

½ teaspoon sea salt

½ cup finely chopped parsley

¼ teaspoon dried oregano

Prepare the polenta: In a blender, process the dry polenta until the granules are very fine. Transfer to a large jar or medium bowl, stir in the water, and refrigerate overnight. This helps the polenta soften and makes it very quick to cook.

Preheat the oven to 425°F and line 2 baking sheets with parchment paper.

Place the broccolini on one sheet and the sweet potato and parsnip on the other. Drizzle the vegetables with olive oil and toss with pinches of salt and pepper. Roast the sweet potato and parsnip for 20 to 25 minutes, or until golden brown around the edges. Roast the broccolini for 10 to 12 minutes.

Make the chimichurri: In a small bowl, combine the olive oil, vinegar, garlic, red pepper flakes, smoked paprika, salt, parsley, and oregano.

Pour the polenta and its soaking water into a medium saucepan. Whisk in the almond milk and the salt and bring to a gentle boil. Reduce the heat to a simmer and cook, whisking occasionally, for 7 to 10 minutes, or until thickened.

Assemble the bowls with a scoop of polenta, the roasted vegetables, drizzles of chimichurri, and drizzles of harissa, if using. Season with salt and pepper to taste. Top with the microgreens, if using, and serve.

SERVES 4

VEGAN & GLUTEN-FREE

ALMOND FLOUR BUCKWHEAT WAFFLES

Despite its name, buckwheat is not wheat. It's not even a grain! It's actually a grain-like seed that contains more protein and nutrients than most wheat-based flours. This recipe happens to be gluten-free, and it's one of my favorites. I recommend using a Belgian waffle maker for these and cooking them a minute or two longer than you would cook other waffles—these are best when the edges are crisp.

———————◆———————

1½ cups almond milk, at room temperature

1½ tablespoons apple cider vinegar

2 tablespoons maple syrup

2 tablespoons melted coconut oil

1 teaspoon vanilla extract

1 cup almond flour

1 cup buckwheat flour

2½ teaspoons baking powder

2 tablespoons ground flaxseed

2 teaspoons cinnamon

½ teaspoon nutmeg

Heaping ¼ teaspoon sea salt

For Serving

Maple syrup

Fruit

Butter or yogurt (optional)

Note: *If you're gluten-free, make sure that the buckwheat and almond flours are both made in certified gluten-free facilities.*

Preheat a waffle iron.

In a medium bowl, stir together the almond milk, apple cider vinegar, maple syrup, coconut oil, and vanilla.

In a large bowl, combine the almond flour, buckwheat flour, baking powder, flaxseed, cinnamon, nutmeg, and salt.

Pour the wet mixture into the bowl of dry ingredients and mix until combined. Let the batter sit for 1 minute to thicken.

Scoop ¾ cup batter for each waffle into a large Belgian waffle maker, or scoop an appropriate amount for your waffle maker. Cook for 5 minutes or according to your waffle maker instructions. I usually cook waffles for 4 minutes, but these need 5 minutes to cook through and get crisp on the outside.

Serve with maple syrup, fruit, and butter or yogurt as desired.

SERVES 4   VEGAN & GLUTEN-FREE

TIP

Make the pickles the day before or up to 2 weeks in advance.

BREAKFAST BANH MI SANDWICHES

There's something just so craveable about a banh mi. It's one of my favorite sandwiches to have for lunch, so I thought, why not make one for breakfast? Instead of a meat or tofu filling, this version has a soft omelet and lemongrass-sautéed mushrooms. The tangy pickles are essential here—for a faster breakfast, make them a few days in advance.

Banh Mi Pickles

1 medium daikon radish, peeled and sliced into matchsticks (7 ounces)

1 small carrot, sliced into matchsticks

1 small Persian cucumber, sliced into matchsticks

½ jalapeño pepper, thinly sliced (optional)

½ cup rice vinegar

Pinch of sugar

Pinch of salt

Sandwiches

2 teaspoons extra-virgin olive oil

8 ounces shiitake mushrooms, stemmed and sliced

1 stalk lemongrass, tender inner part, minced

1 teaspoon rice vinegar

6 large eggs, beaten

4 (5-inch) soft ciabatta rolls or baguette pieces

Mayo, for slathering

Sriracha, for drizzling

½ cup fresh cilantro, coarsely chopped

Sea salt

Make the banh mi pickles: Place the daikon, carrot, cucumber, and jalapeño, if using, into a tightly lidded jar just large enough to hold all the vegetables. Add the rice vinegar, sugar, and salt and shake gently. If necessary, add water so that the liquid just covers the vegetables and shake again. Gently pack the vegetables down into the jar and chill for at least 1 hour. Store in the fridge for up to 2 weeks.

Prepare the sandwiches: In a medium skillet, heat the olive oil over medium heat. Add the mushrooms and a pinch of salt and toss to coat. Cook until browned and tender, 6 to 8 minutes, stirring only occasionally. Stir in the lemongrass, and then the rice vinegar. Transfer the mushrooms to a plate and set aside.

In a large nonstick skillet over medium heat, pour in half of the beaten eggs and sprinkle with salt. Cook until the center begins to set, about 2 minutes. Fold the omelet in thirds to create a long rectangular shape. Leave the omelet in the warm pan for 30 more seconds, or until the eggs are set. Remove from the pan and repeat with the remaining eggs to make a second omelet. Cut both omelets in half horizontally.

To assemble the sandwiches, slice the ciabatta rolls lengthwise, but not all the way through.

Spread mayo on one side of the bread and add a drizzle of sriracha. Top with an omelet half, the mushrooms, banh mi pickles, and the cilantro. Serve with more sriracha on the side, if desired.

SERVES 4

VEGAN: Double the mushrooms, skip the egg, and use vegan mayo.

SWEET POTATO & SAGE BREAKFAST BISCUITS

Here's how cooking in our relationship goes: I do most of it, but Jack loves to get his hands (and the floor) messy with baking projects. He's fanatical about biscuits, and I'm a superfan of sweet potatoes, so if I had to choose a recipe that represents our relationship, it would probably be this one. Serve with scrambled eggs or scrambled tofu for a balanced breakfast, or with jam as an afternoon snack. These are best just out of the oven, but they also freeze well.

❖

¾ cup soft sweet potato flesh, chilled*

⅓ cup almond milk

1 teaspoon apple cider vinegar

2 cups all-purpose flour, plus more for working with the dough

1 tablespoon cane sugar

1 tablespoon baking powder

½ teaspoon baking soda

½ teaspoon sea salt

¼ cup plus 1 tablespoon coconut oil, hardened and cut into small pieces**

8 to 10 fresh sage leaves

1 teaspoon melted coconut oil, for brushing

*To prepare the sweet potato: Use a fork to poke holes in 1 medium sweet potato and roast in a 425°F oven for 60 minutes, or until soft. Scoop out the soft flesh and chill before adding to the dough.

**Coconut oil is easiest to work with if you measure it while it's soft and then place it in a small bowl and freeze for 15 minutes. Use a paring knife to cut into small pieces.

Preheat the oven to 425°F and line a baking sheet with parchment paper.

In a small bowl, stir together the sweet potato flesh, almond milk, and apple cider vinegar.

In a food processor, place the flour, sugar, baking powder, baking soda, and salt and pulse several times to combine. Add the hardened coconut oil and sage leaves and pulse a few times until the coconut oil is just combined. Add the sweet potato mixture and process until the dough forms a ball. Remove the dough from the food processor and place on a floured surface. Knead lightly, using more flour as needed to prevent sticking, and flatten into a disk about ¾ inch thick. Use a small glass or a 2- to 3-inch round biscuit cutter and cut out the biscuits. Form scraps into another small disk and cut out the remaining dough.

Place the biscuits on the baking sheet, brush with the melted coconut oil, and bake for 12 to 13 minutes or until puffed up and golden brown.

MAKES 9 TO 12 BISCUITS   VEGAN

VEGAN: Instead of the eggs, combine 2 tablespoons ground flaxseed and 2 tablespoons water and set aside to thicken for 5 minutes before adding to the wet ingredients.

APPLE CINNAMON OAT MUFFINS

A good week for me starts with a stash of these muffins in the freezer. With their soft texture and the flavors of nutmeg and cinnamon in mind, I'm eager to start my day. These aren't your big, cakey bakery muffins; instead, they're delightful everyday muffins that you can feel good about eating (two of) for breakfast.

1¼ cups Homemade Oat Flour (page 61)

½ cup almond flour

¼ cup arrowroot starch

2 teaspoons cinnamon

½ teaspoon nutmeg

1 teaspoon baking powder

½ teaspoon baking soda

½ teaspoon sea salt

2 large eggs

⅔ cup almond milk

⅓ cup maple syrup

⅓ cup extra-virgin olive oil

1 tablespoon apple cider vinegar

1 teaspoon vanilla extract

1 cup finely diced apple, plus slices for garnish

½ cup walnuts, chopped

¼ cup gluten-free whole rolled oats, for garnish (optional)

Preheat the oven to 350°F and lightly grease or spray a 12-cup muffin tin.

In a large bowl, combine the oat flour, almond flour, arrowroot, cinnamon, nutmeg, baking powder, baking soda, and salt.

In a medium bowl, whisk together the eggs, almond milk, maple syrup, olive oil, apple cider vinegar, and vanilla.

Pour the wet ingredients into the bowl of dry ingredients and stir until just combined. Do not overmix. Stir in the diced apple and walnuts. Use a ⅓-cup measuring scoop to divide the batter into the muffin tin. Garnish with the sliced apple and oats, if desired.

Bake for 18 minutes, or until the tops slightly spring back to the touch. Cool for 10 minutes, then remove from the pan and place on a wire rack to finish cooling.

MAKES 12 MUFFINS

GLUTEN-FREE

TIP   **WHOLE WHEAT VERSION:** Use 1¾ cups whole wheat pastry flour (or white-wheat mix) instead of oat flour, almond flour, and arrowroot starch.

PEACHY OVERNIGHT OATS

It took me a while to get on the overnight oats bandwagon due to the one year in college when I ate oatmeal for breakfast, lunch, and sometimes dinner, every single day (hey, it was cheap!). Only recently did I give overnight oats a chance, and I love them! Their texture is less mushy than stovetop hot oats and also less mushy than my college microwaved oats. Topped with juicy peaches and crispy granola, this breakfast makes me excited to wake up in the morning.

◆—◆

1 cup gluten-free whole rolled oats

1 cup almond milk

¼ teaspoon cinnamon

1 ripe peach, pitted and diced

Maple syrup, for drizzling (optional)

Granola (makes extra)

1 cup gluten-free whole rolled oats

¼ cup chopped walnuts

1 teaspoon cinnamon

¼ teaspoon sea salt

1 tablespoon melted coconut oil

2 tablespoons maple syrup

1 tablespoon creamy almond butter

Divide the oats, almond milk, and cinnamon between 2 (16-ounce) jars and stir to combine. Chill overnight.

Make the granola: Preheat the oven to 300°F and line a baking sheet with parchment paper.

In a medium bowl, combine the oats, walnuts, cinnamon, and salt. Drizzle in the coconut oil and maple syrup and add the almond butter. Stir until combined. Scoop the granola onto the baking sheet and press the mixture into a 1-inch-thick circle. This will encourage clumping. Bake for 15 minutes, rotate the pan halfway, and use a fork to gently break the granola apart just a bit. Bake 15 minutes more or until golden brown. Let cool for 15 minutes before serving.

In the morning, top the oats in each jar with half of the peach, 1 tablespoon of granola, and a drizzle of maple syrup, if desired. Store extra granola in an airtight container.

SERVES 2

VEGAN & GLUTEN-FREE

TIP Make this with apples in the fall, strawberries or raspberries in the spring, or frozen fruit anytime of year!

HOW TO MAKE SOFT-BOILED EGGS

1.

Fill a medium pot with water and heat to a gentle simmer, just below boiling. Using a slotted spoon, carefully lower the eggs into the water and let simmer for 7 minutes.

2.

Remove and chill immediately in a bowl of ice water for 3 minutes.

3.

Once the eggs are cool, tap the bottom of each egg to crack a little bit of the shell.

4.

Take a small spoon and carefully slide it in and around the egg to loosen and remove it from the shell.

HOW TO MAKE POACHED EGGS

Crack the first egg into a small bowl.

Heat a medium pot of water until bubbles form on the bottom of the pan but the water is not yet boiling. Add a few splashes of white vinegar. Stir the water so that it moves in a circular motion.

Gently drop the egg into the water, give the water one more gentle stir, then set a timer for 4 minutes.

Scoop the egg out of the water. Test the egg for doneness and determine if you need more or less time per egg. Continue with the remaining eggs. If you're comfortable with the technique, you can poach two at a time!

HOMEMADE OAT FLOUR

There's no need to go out and buy packaged oat flour when you can blend it yourself!

1.
Place whole rolled oats in a food processor.

2.
Blend until the oats become a fine flour, stopping to stir occasionally.

3.
Store in an airtight container in a cool, dry place.

Use in these recipes that call for oat flour:
Banana Bread Quinoa Breakfast Cookies, page 35
Apple Cinnamon Oat Muffins, page 57
Vegan Date Brownies, page 245
Peanut Butter Snickerdoodles, page 251

1 cup whole rolled oats yields about ¾ cup oat flour.

6 WAYS TO SCRAMBLE

—— EACH RECIPE SERVES *2* ——

BASE INSTRUCTIONS: Beat 4 large eggs in a bowl with pinches of sea salt and freshly ground black pepper. Following each recipe's instructions, use a rubber spatula to fold and scramble the eggs. Tip: Remove eggs from the pan while they're still slightly runny for a creamy, soft scramble.

Season the finished eggs with salt and pepper to taste!

1 MIGAS

Heat ½ **teaspoon olive oil** in a small skillet. Sauté **2 tablespoons diced red onion** for 1 minute, then add the eggs. Fold in ¼ **cup Quick Pico** (page 305) and scramble. Transfer to plates and top with ¼ **cup baked tortilla strips** and **chopped cilantro**.

2 MUSHROOM MEDLEY

Heat ½ **teaspoon olive oil** in a small skillet over medium heat. Add the eggs, then **1 cup sliced sautéed mushrooms**. Scramble, then transfer to plates and garnish with **chopped tarragon** and **chives**.

3

SPRING GREEN

Whisk ¼ teaspoon **Dijon mustard** into the beaten egg mixture. Heat ½ **teaspoon olive oil** in a small skillet and sauté ½ **cup chopped asparagus** for 2 minutes. Add the eggs and scramble. Transfer to plates and garnish with **fresh dill** and a few **pea shoots**.

4

FALL HARVEST

Heat ½ **teaspoon olive oil** in a small skillet. Add **2 tablespoons chopped scallions** and sauté for 1 minute. Add the eggs, then fold in ½ **cup roasted sweet potato cubes** and **1 tablespoon chopped sage**. Scramble, then top with ¼ **cup crumbled feta cheese**.

5

SUPER GREEN

Heat ½ **teaspoon olive oil** in a small skillet over medium heat. Add **2 tablespoons chopped scallions** and ½ **cup finely chopped kale** and sauté for 2 minutes. Add the eggs, scramble, then transfer to plates and top with **mint pesto** (page 303) and **microgreens**.

6 SOUTHWEST SCRAMBLE

Heat ½ **teaspoon olive oil** in a small skillet over medium heat. Add **2 tablespoons diced red onion**, ¼ **cup chopped bell pepper**, and ¼ **cup cooked black beans** (page 23) and sauté for 2 minutes. Add the eggs, scramble, then top with **diced avocado** and a **squeeze of lime**.

SNA & STA

CKS
RTERS

ZUCCHINI & RADISH CARPACCIO CROSTINI

In my line of work, I get asked these two questions the most: "What the heck is a food blog?" and "Where do you find those pretty radishes?" If you're reading this book, you already know the answer to number one. The answer to question two is that you're likely already walking past them at your regular store or farmers market! On the outside, watermelon and daikon radishes are easy to overlook— they're grubby, dull-colored, and oddly shaped. Keep an eye out for them in the spring or fall; otherwise, use red radishes here—they're equally delicious when thinly sliced and marinated in this zippy lemon-ginger dressing.

Lemon-Ginger Dressing

2 tablespoons extra-virgin olive oil

1 tablespoon fresh lemon juice

1 tablespoon white wine vinegar

1 teaspoon minced ginger

½ garlic clove, minced

¼ teaspoon maple syrup

¼ teaspoon sea salt

Freshly ground black pepper

Crostini

6 small watermelon radishes and/or purple daikon radishes

1 small zucchini

1 scallion, very thinly sliced

1 baguette, warmed and sliced diagonally ⅓ inch thick

8 ounces goat cheese, Lemon Zest Labneh (page 295), or Almond Cheese (page 73)

Flaky sea salt

Microgreens, for garnish (optional)

Make the lemon-ginger dressing: In the bottom of a large bowl, whisk together the olive oil, lemon juice, vinegar, ginger, garlic, maple syrup, salt, and several grinds of pepper.

With a mandoline or a sharp knife, thinly slice the radishes and zucchini into rounds. I like to use a mandoline to get very thin, uniform slices.

Add the radish and zucchini slices and the scallion to the bowl and toss to coat. Assemble the crostini by layering baguette slices with the goat cheese, labneh, or almond cheese; a few pieces of each vegetable; and pinches of flaky sea salt. Top with microgreens, if desired.

SERVES 4 TO 6   VEGAN: Use Almond Cheese.   GLUTEN-FREE: Use gluten-free bread.

CARROT GINGER GYOZA DUMPLINGS

After our first trip to Japan, Jack could not stop talking about gyoza and about how much he wanted to (er . . . how much he wanted *me* to) make them at home. With a little help from pre-made gyoza wrappers, we started making dumplings regularly, with all types of various fillings. The compromise was that I'd make the filling and he would do the wrapping. He still doesn't know that I gave myself the easier job, so don't tell him, okay?

4 medium carrots (8 ounces)

½ teaspoon extra-virgin olive oil, plus more for drizzling

3½ ounces extra-firm tofu

2 teaspoons white miso paste

2 teaspoons rice vinegar

1 teaspoon minced ginger

1 garlic clove

½ teaspoon sesame oil

½ teaspoon sriracha

2 tablespoons sliced scallions

30 store-bought dumpling wrappers

Tamari, for dipping

Sea salt and freshly ground black pepper

Preheat the oven to 425°F and line a baking sheet with parchment paper. Place the carrots on the baking sheet, drizzle lightly with olive oil, and sprinkle with salt and pepper. Roast for 15 to 25 minutes, or until browned and soft. The time will depend on the thickness of the carrots.

Remove the carrots from the oven, let cool slightly, then chop and transfer to a small food processor. Add the olive oil, tofu, miso paste, rice vinegar, ginger, garlic, sesame oil, and sriracha and pulse to combine. The carrots should be fairly well pureed, and the mixture will be thick. Stir in the scallions.

Assemble the dumplings by scooping 1 heaping teaspoon of filling onto each wrapper. Using your fingers, dab the edges of the wrapper with cold water, fold in half over the filling, and press to seal. With the wrapper folded in half and while holding the top of the crescent with two fingers, use the other hand to fold pleats.

Lightly spray the racks of a bamboo steamer with cooking spray. Place the dumplings in the bamboo steamer without touching each other and cover with the lid. Bring 1 inch of water to a simmer in a pot or skillet that the steamer can hover over. Place the bamboo steamer on top and steam for 10 minutes. Serve with tamari for dipping.

MAKES ABOUT 30 DUMPLINGS. SERVES 4 TO 6 | VEGAN

BEET MUHAMMARA DIP

I remember the first time I had muhammara, a spiced Middle Eastern red pepper walnut dip. I loved the bold flavors and the fragrant coriander scent. It reminded me so much of the way I like to season my beet hummus, so I thought, "Why not beet muhammara?" It's not only a fun twist, but also the sweetness of the beets along with a little extra lemon replace the hard-to-find pomegranate molasses, making this version more approachable and every bit as delectable.

---

10 ounces red beets (2 to 3 beets)

1 small shallot

1 large garlic clove, unpeeled

1 teaspoon whole cumin seeds

¾ cup walnuts, plus more for garnish

2 tablespoons fresh lemon juice

½ teaspoon red pepper flakes, or to taste

½ teaspoon ground coriander

½ teaspoon sea salt, plus more to taste

¼ cup extra-virgin olive oil, plus more for drizzling

Freshly ground black pepper

Toasted pita or veggies, for serving

Sesame seeds (optional)

Mint (optional)

Preheat the oven to 425°F. Wrap the beets in foil with a drizzle of olive oil and a pinch of salt and pepper. Wrap the shallot and garlic in another piece of foil with a drizzle of olive oil, salt, and pepper. Place both packages on a baking sheet and roast the shallot and garlic for 25 to 30 minutes, or until very soft. Roast the beets for 60 minutes, or until fork-tender. Remove the beets from the oven and unwrap the foil. When they are cool to the touch, peel the skins. I like to hold them under running water and slide the skins off with my hands. Chop the beets. Peel the garlic.

In a small skillet, toast the cumin seeds over medium-low heat until lightly browned and fragrant, about 1 minute. Remove the cumin from the skillet, then add the walnuts and lightly toast them for 30 seconds to 1 minute.

In a food processor, place the beets, shallot, garlic, cumin, walnuts, lemon juice, red pepper flakes, coriander, salt, and a few grinds of black pepper and process until combined. With the blade running, drizzle in the ¼ cup olive oil and blend until smooth.

Season to taste and serve with toasted pita or veggies. Garnish with a drizzle of olive oil, walnuts, sesame seeds, and mint, if desired.

MAKES 2 CUPS

VEGAN & GLUTEN-FREE

TIP Even though roasting beets is a hands-off task, it's time-consuming, so I like to do it ahead of time. The beets, shallot, and garlic can be roasted up to a day in advance and stored in the fridge.

ALMOND CHEESE WITH HERBES DE PROVENCE

Making nut cheese may seem fussy, but it's really not. Blend the ingredients, wrap them in cheesecloth, wait two days (the hard part!), then unwrap your "cheese." I like to top mine with a sprinkle of herbes de Provence and a bit of mint for freshness. If you absolutely cannot wait two days for your "cheese," just serve the mixture as a dip—it's creamy and delicious either way!

1½ cups slivered almonds

3 tablespoons fresh lemon juice

1 tablespoon nutritional yeast

1 tablespoon extra-virgin olive oil

1 small garlic clove

½ teaspoon sea salt

½ cup water, plus more if needed

½ teaspoon herbes de Provence

2 mint leaves, minced (optional)

Flaky sea salt, for sprinkling

Crackers and/or veggies, for serving

In a blender, place the almonds, lemon juice, nutritional yeast, olive oil, garlic, salt, and water and process until smooth. If the mixture is too thick to blend, add more water, 1 tablespoon at a time, until it blends to a smooth, yet still very thick, consistency.

Scoop the mixture onto a layer of cheesecloth. Bring the edges of the cheesecloth together, tie it around a wooden spoon, and place the spoon across the top of a large bowl so that the cheese ball hangs in the center but does not touch the bottom of the bowl. Chill for 48 hours or until the cheese is a soft yet cohesive ball. The ball should pull away from the cheesecloth when carefully unwrapped. If it's sticking to the cheesecloth too much, wrap it back up and chill for another 24 hours.

Transfer the cheese ball to a serving plate and gently press down to form into a disk. Sprinkle with the herbes de Provence, the mint, if using, and the flaky sea salt. Serve with crackers and veggies.

MAKES 1½ CUPS

VEGAN & GLUTEN-FREE

TIP This recipe makes a lot of dip, but I promise, if you serve it at a party, it'll go quick! Store any leftover queso in the fridge—it will last 4 to 5 days. It's great served warm or chilled.

LOADED BUTTERNUT SQUASH QUESO

As soon as I graduated from college, I moved to Austin (aka the land of queso) to be with Jack. Whenever we'd get together with friends, there would always be queso, which was often the too-yellow, too-fake type of cheese that I don't exactly gravitate toward. I couldn't really complain because I'd fill up on chips, salsa, and guacamole instead . . . but now I can have the best of both worlds with this oozy butternut queso loaded with all the toppings. Even though this recipe is vegan, every cheese lover I know loves this dip.

---

2 cups peeled and diced Yukon Gold potatoes

1 cup peeled and diced butternut squash

½ cup chopped yellow onion

½ cup raw cashews

¼ cup extra-virgin olive oil, plus more for drizzling

¼ cup plus 2 tablespoons water

¼ cup nutritional yeast

¼ cup fresh lemon juice

2 tablespoons apple cider vinegar

2 garlic cloves

1 teaspoon smoked paprika

½ teaspoon cayenne pepper

1 teaspoon sea salt

For Serving

1 avocado

Juice of ½ lime

Pinches of sea salt

¼ cup cooked black beans, drained and rinsed (page 23)

¼ cup diced tomato

2 tablespoons diced red onion

1 small jalapeño pepper, diced

¼ cup chopped fresh cilantro

Tortilla chips

Place the diced potatoes and butternut squash in a medium saucepan and cover with cold water by about 1 inch. Add a pinch of salt. Bring to a boil, then reduce the heat and simmer, uncovered, until fork-tender, 8 to 12 minutes. Drain and transfer to a high-speed blender.

In a small skillet over medium heat, sauté the onion in a drizzle of olive oil until soft, about 5 minutes.

To the blender, add the sautéed onion, cashews, the ¼ cup olive oil, water, nutritional yeast, lemon juice, apple cider vinegar, garlic, smoked paprika, cayenne, and salt. Blend until smooth, using the blender baton to help keep the blade moving or pausing to stir as necessary. If the mixture is too thick, add more water, 1 tablespoon at a time, and blend until smooth.

Make a quick guacamole by mashing together the avocado, lime juice, and sea salt in a small bowl with the back of a fork.

Scoop the warm queso into a shallow serving dish and top with the guacamole, black beans, diced tomato, red onion, jalapeño, and cilantro. Serve with tortilla chips.

SERVES 4

VEGAN & GLUTEN-FREE

EVERYDAY SESAME BROWN RICE CRACKERS

My obsession with shopping the bulk bins started young. Growing up, my mom would take my sister and me to a tiny bulk food store in our neighborhood where she bought spices from the bulk bins and never ever in expensive little jars. As a treat, we'd always leave with a bag full of sesame sticks that we'd eat in the car (and later sneak into movie theaters). These crackers remind me of those sesame sticks and, by extension, my entire childhood. This version, which is entirely gluten-free, is more subtle than those sesame sticks were, but still has a wonderful sesame flavor that comes from the toasted sesame oil.

❖

½ cup brown rice flour

½ cup almond flour

¼ cup plus 2 tablespoons sesame seeds

2 tablespoons ground flaxseed

¼ teaspoon baking powder

½ teaspoon sea salt

1 teaspoon sesame oil

¼ cup water

Preheat the oven to 350°F.

In a medium bowl, combine the brown rice flour, almond flour, sesame seeds, flaxseed, baking powder, and salt. Add the sesame oil and water and stir. The mixture will be very crumbly. Use your hands to press and knead it together to form a cohesive ball. Form the ball into a disk and place it between 2 sheets of parchment paper on a flat surface. Roll the dough into an oval shape about ⅛ inch thick. If the edges start to tear, use your fingers to gently press them back together.

Remove the top sheet of parchment paper and use a sharp paring knife to score the crackers into approximately 2-inch squares. Some dough around the edges will be irregular in shape. Gently lift the parchment paper with the dough and transfer it to a baking sheet. Bake for 25 minutes, or until golden brown around the edges. Remove the pan from the oven and let sit for 10 minutes. Break the crackers apart.

MAKES ABOUT 16 CRACKERS

VEGAN & GLUTEN-FREE

TIP These freeze very well—I like to have them on hand at all times!

JACK'S GARLIC PRETZEL KNOTS

Around here, Jack is the dough man. He's soft, pillowy, and malleable (don't worry—this headnote is Jack-approved!). Oh, and he also likes to make recipes that involve dough, so there's that. There's nothing quite like the smell of baking bread wafting out of the oven—especially when you've got a kind-hearted loved one to make it for you. He loves to make these when we're having friends over for dinner. If there are any leftover, they freeze well!

❖

¾ cup warm water (105°F to 115°F)

1 tablespoon maple syrup

1 (¼-ounce) package active dry yeast

1½ cups all-purpose flour, plus more for kneading

½ cup whole wheat flour

1 teaspoon sea salt

4 tablespoons extra-virgin olive oil, plus more for brushing

1 garlic clove, minced

¼ teaspoon lemon zest

Coarse salt, for sprinkling

In a small bowl, stir together ¼ cup of the water, maple syrup, and the yeast. Set aside for 5 minutes, until the yeast is foamy.

In the bowl of a mixer fitted with a dough hook, place the flours and salt. Add the yeast mixture, 2 tablespoons of the olive oil, and the remaining ½ cup of water. Mix on medium speed until the dough forms a ball around the hook, 5 to 6 minutes. Turn the dough out onto a lightly floured surface and knead several times, sprinkling with more flour, as needed, and form into a ball. Brush a large bowl with olive oil, and place the dough inside. Cover with plastic wrap and set aside to rise until doubled in size, 40 to 60 minutes.

Preheat the oven to 450°F and line a baking sheet with parchment paper. Uncover the dough, punch it down and transfer to a lightly floured surface. Cut the dough into 8 equal sections, and roll each section into a 9-inch-long rope. Grab the ends of each dough rope, tie into a knot, and tuck in the ends.

In a small bowl, combine the remaining 2 tablespoons olive oil, the garlic, and lemon zest. Set aside.

Bake the pretzel knots for 10 to 12 minutes, or until golden brown. Brush the garlic oil onto the hot pretzel knots and sprinkle each with coarse salt.

MAKES 8 PRETZEL KNOTS   VEGAN

ANATOMY OF A
SNACK

NUT & SEED MIXES

Base Instructions: Preheat the oven to 350°F and line 3 small baking sheets with parchment paper. Combine ingredients for each mix, making sure the nuts/seeds are well coated. Spread into a thin layer and bake 8 to 12 minutes or until lightly toasted.

Rosemary Roasted Almonds

¾ cup raw almonds
½ teaspoon extra-virgin olive oil
½ teaspoon maple syrup
½ tablespoon minced rosemary
Pinches of sea salt

Spicy Pepitas

½ cup pepitas
½ teaspoon tamari
¼ teaspoon chili powder
Pinch of cayenne pepper

Coconut Curried Cashews

¾ cup raw cashews
½ teaspoon melted coconut oil
½ teaspoon maple syrup
½ teaspoon curry powder
2 tablespoons dried currants
2 tablespoons coconut flakes
Pinches of sea salt

CHEESES

Sliced Hard Cheese

For example, manchego or aged white cheddar

Soft Cheese

For example, brie, goat cheese, or Almond Cheese (page 73)

BOARD

Choose as few or as many components as you want to make your own customized appetizer platter!

SOMETHING SWEET

Fig & Thyme Butter with Baguette
½ cup unsalted butter, at room temperature
2 dried figs, diced
1½ teaspoons fresh thyme leaves
1½ teaspoons maple syrup
Pinches of sea salt
Sliced baguette, for serving

Combine the butter, dried figs, thyme, maple syrup, and salt in a food processor and process until smooth.

A CREAMY DIP WITH FRESH VEGGIES

For example, Radish-Green Goddess Dip (page 302).

Any raw or blanched vegetables you like!

So

UPS

TIP

I like to store fresh ginger in the freezer to have it on hand at all times. When ready to use, no need to thaw—just grate it frozen!

COCONUT SOUP WITH SWEET POTATO & KALE

The first time I had tom kha, I exclaimed, "I want to eat this every day!" And I did. For dinner, for a takeout lunch, and for dinner the next day. I was obsessed with the rich, creamy, tangy coconut soup. It's usually made with a host of hard-to-find ingredients, so I simplified it. This vegan version, made without fish sauce, gets its complex flavor from cilantro stems (there's actually more flavor in the stems than the leaves), ginger, lemongrass, and serrano chiles. I bulk it up with sweet potatoes and a few handfuls of kale, which isn't traditional but is filling and delicious.

---

2 stalks lemongrass

1 teaspoon coconut oil

½ medium yellow onion, thinly sliced

12 ounces cremini mushrooms, stemmed and sliced

½ to 1 teaspoon sea salt

2 (14-ounce) cans full-fat coconut milk

1½ cups water (up to 3 cups for lighter broth)

1 tablespoon minced fresh ginger

2 garlic cloves, minced

1 large sweet potato, chopped

1 jalapeño pepper, stemmed and diced

1 small bunch cilantro, stems diced (½ cup), leaves chopped

Zest and juice of 2 limes

Tamari, for seasoning (optional)

4 cups loosely packed kale, chopped

2 cups cooked jasmine rice (page 22)

½ cup fresh mint leaves

Sliced red chile peppers, serrano peppers, or sriracha

Prepare the lemongrass by cutting off the root end and the tough upper stem of the stalks. Smash the stalks with a rolling pin to loosen the layers. Pull off the thick outer layers and dice the inner, tender parts. This should yield about ¼ cup chopped lemongrass. Set aside.

Heat the oil in a large pot over medium heat. Add the onion, mushrooms, and ½ teaspoon salt and cook, stirring occasionally, for 8 minutes, or until softened.

Stir in the lemongrass, coconut milk, 1½ cups water, ginger, garlic, sweet potato, jalapeño, and cilantro stems. If you prefer a lighter broth, add up to 1½ cups more water. Simmer over low heat for 20 minutes, or until the sweet potatoes are fork-tender.

Add the lime zest and juice. Taste, then add an additional ½ teaspoon of salt, if desired, and tamari, if using. Add the chopped kale and simmer just until wilted, 1 to 2 minutes. Stir in the cilantro leaves just before serving.

Serve with the rice, fresh mint, and chile peppers, if using, and tamari on the side.

SERVES 4 TO 6

VEGAN & GLUTEN-FREE

SHEET PAN SQUASH SOUP

To me, butternut squash soup is the ultimate fall comfort food: its rich, creamy texture and bold color brighten up cool days. Over the years I've streamlined my recipe. I simply roast the vegetables on a sheet pan and blend them with broth, miso, and a splash of vinegar for a soothing bowl of soup.

◆

1 (2-pound) butternut squash

1 small yellow onion

3 tablespoons extra-virgin olive oil

5 unpeeled garlic cloves

2 cups Vegetable Broth (page 104)

1½ tablespoons white miso paste

1 teaspoon white wine vinegar

Sea salt and freshly ground black pepper

Coconut milk, for garnish (optional)

Preheat the oven to 400°F and line a baking sheet with parchment paper.

Cut the squash in half and scoop out the seeds. Cut the onion into quarters. Place the squash and the onion on the baking sheet and drizzle with 1 tablespoon of the olive oil and pinches of salt and pepper. Arrange the squash and onions cut-side down. Wrap the garlic in foil and place on the baking sheet. Roast for 40 to 50 minutes, or until the squash is soft and the onion is nicely browned.

Scoop the flesh from the squash and place in a blender with the onion, peeled garlic, vegetable broth, miso paste, vinegar, and the remaining 2 tablespoons olive oil. Blend until creamy, about 1 minute. Season to taste with salt and pepper.

Serve with a drizzle of olive oil and a spoonful of coconut milk, if using.

SERVES 4

VEGAN & GLUTEN-FREE

LEMON MISO SPRING GREEN SOUP

Cleanse-style diets are not my style. If you tell me I can't have a cookie, all I will be able to think about are cookies, and then I'll end up eating a whole batch of cookies. Diet: failed. Instead, whenever I feel like I need a healthful reset, I make this soup. It's chock-full of green vegetables, and the broth is simple but oh so flavorful thanks to miso paste, lemon, and a good dose of freshly cracked black pepper.

2 tablespoons extra-virgin olive oil

1 bunch scallions, sliced (1 cup)

2 garlic cloves, minced

4 cups Vegetable Broth (page 104)

4 cups water

½ cup uncooked quinoa

10 fresh thyme sprigs, bundled

½ teaspoon sea salt, plus more to taste

¼ cup white miso paste

1 cup snap peas, stringed and sliced lengthwise

1 cup chopped asparagus, tender parts

½ cup fresh or frozen peas

½ cup cooked chickpeas, drained and rinsed (page 23)

6 lacinato kale leaves, chopped, stems diced

¼ teaspoon freshly ground black pepper

¼ cup fresh lemon juice

¼ cup chopped fresh dill, half reserved for garnish

1 recipe Mint Pesto (page 303)

Heat the oil in a large pot over medium heat. Add the scallions and cook for 3 minutes, then stir in the garlic, vegetable broth, water, quinoa, thyme, ¼ teaspoon of the salt, and a few grinds of black pepper. Bring to a boil, then reduce the heat and simmer, covered, for 20 minutes until the quinoa is cooked.

In a small bowl, whisk the miso paste with ½ cup of the hot cooking broth, then stir the mixture back into the simmering pot.

Stir in the snap peas, asparagus, peas, chickpeas, and kale and simmer until the vegetables are tender but still vibrant green, 3 to 4 minutes. Season with the remaining ¼ teaspoon salt and the black pepper. Stir in the lemon juice and half of the dill.

Portion the soup into bowls and top with the remaining fresh dill. Serve with the mint pesto.

SERVES 4 TO 6   VEGAN & GLUTEN-FREE

VEGAN POTATO, LEEK & ARTICHOKE CHOWDER

I did a poll on Instagram one day where I asked what soups people would like me to make. I love *all* soups, but sometimes I suffer from soup indecision. There was an overwhelming number of requests for chowders and leek soups, so . . . request granted. This potato leek chowder gets its creaminess from potatoes and blended cashews. With a nice pop of flavor from the briny artichokes and capers, it's most delicious finished with a little lemon juice and fresh dill.

———◆———

2 tablespoons extra-virgin olive oil, plus more for drizzling

3 leeks, white and light green parts, thinly sliced and rinsed (3½ cups)

½ cup chopped celery

½ cup chopped carrots

½ teaspoon sea salt, plus more to taste

Freshly ground black pepper

3 garlic cloves, minced

1½ pounds Yukon Gold potatoes, chopped

4 cups Vegetable Broth (page 104)

1 (14-ounce) can artichoke hearts, drained and chopped

½ cup raw cashews

1½ teaspoons Dijon mustard

1 tablespoon capers

3 tablespoons fresh lemon juice

½ to 1 cup water

¼ cup fresh dill, plus more for garnish

¼ cup chopped chives

Heat the oil in a large pot over medium heat. Add the leeks, celery, carrots, the salt, and a few grinds of black pepper. Sauté, stirring occasionally, until the vegetables begin to soften, 8 to 10 minutes, turning down the heat if they start to over-brown.

Add the garlic and sauté for 1 minute more. Add the potatoes and the broth. Bring to a boil, then reduce the heat and simmer for 15 to 20 minutes, or until the potatoes are tender. Stir in the artichokes.

Let cool slightly, then transfer one-third of the soup to a blender along with the cashews, mustard, capers, and 1 tablespoon of the lemon juice. Puree until smooth, and then pour the mixture back into the soup pot. Stir in the water, as desired, to thin. Add the dill and the remaining 2 tablespoons lemon juice. Season to taste with more salt and pepper and serve.

Garnish with more dill, the chives, and a drizzle of olive oil.

Leftover soup can be stored in the fridge for 3 to 4 days. Avoid freezing.

SERVES 6

VEGAN & GLUTEN-FREE

LASAGNA SOUP WITH VEGAN RICOTTA

When you feel like lasagna, but you don't feel like *making* lasagna, what do you do? Make lasagna soup, of course! This has a delicious, saucy tomato base; broken-up lasagna noodles; and dollops of rich vegan ricotta. To make this easier to eat, you can break up the noodles even more, but I think it's fun to eat through the big, curly, sloppy noodles!

———◆———

2 tablespoons extra-virgin olive oil, plus more for drizzling

1 medium yellow onion, diced

2 medium carrots, chopped

1 fennel bulb, diced

½ teaspoon sea salt, plus more to taste

Freshly ground black pepper

2 teaspoons balsamic vinegar

2 garlic cloves, minced

1 (28-ounce) can diced tomatoes

3½ cups water

12 fresh thyme sprigs, bundled, or 1 tablespoon fresh thyme leaves

¼ to ½ teaspoon red pepper flakes

8 lasagna noodles, broken into halves or thirds

8 cups fresh spinach

1 cup Vegan Ricotta (page 285)

½ cup chopped fresh parsley or basil

Microgreens (optional)

Heat the oil in a large pot over medium heat. Add the onion, carrots, fennel, salt, and a few grinds of black pepper and cook, stirring, until the vegetables begin to soften, about 8 minutes. Add the balsamic vinegar, garlic, tomatoes, water, thyme, and red pepper flakes. Cover and simmer for 30 minutes, or until the vegetables are tender.

Meanwhile, cook the lasagna noodles in a pot of salted boiling water according to the package directions until al dente. Drain and toss with a tiny bit of olive oil to keep the noodles from sticking together.

Add the spinach and the lasagna noodles to the soup and stir until the spinach is wilted. Remove the thyme bundle and season to taste with more salt and pepper, if desired.

Serve in bowls with scoops of the ricotta and sprinkle with fresh parsley. Garnish with microgreens, if desired.

SERVES 4 TO 6

VEGAN | GLUTEN-FREE: Use gluten-free noodles.

HOW TO FREEZE HERBS

Herbs are essential for adding freshness and flavor to dishes, but in Chicago's cold climate, they don't grow in the wintertime. While I always prefer to cook with fresh herbs, it's surprising how much flavor frozen herbs can add to winter soups and stews! Hearty herbs like rosemary and thyme freeze best because they don't wilt, but frozen cilantro is wonderful in my Coconut Soup with Sweet Potato & Kale (page 85). In the Versatile Vegetable Lentil Soup (page 103), frozen parsley is a great addition, and if you don't have fresh basil on hand, frozen basil will round out the Lasagna Soup with Vegan Ricotta (page 93).

1.

Clip fresh herbs. Wash and dry them well.

2.

Place in freezer-safe bags or containers with a paper towel to soak up any remaining moisture as they freeze.

3.

To use, chop frozen herbs with a knife or use your hands to crunch and crumble softer herbs.

PARSNIP CHICKPEA NOODLE SOUP

There are some days when I just crave a comforting bowl of chicken noodle soup. Since chickpeas are my chicken, I turn to this soup for that comfort. It has a hearty mix of vegetables, fresh thyme, dried sage (which is the secret to chicken-like flavor), and brown rice elbow noodles.

---

2 tablespoons extra-virgin olive oil

1 medium yellow onion, chopped

3 medium carrots, chopped

1 medium parsnip, chopped

3 medium celery stalks, thinly sliced

½ teaspoon sea salt, plus more to taste

½ teaspoon freshly ground black pepper

3 large garlic cloves, minced

8 cups Vegetable Broth (page 104)

15 fresh thyme sprigs, bundled

½ teaspoon dried sage

2 tablespoons tomato paste

1½ cups cooked chickpeas, drained and rinsed (page 23)

6 ounces brown rice elbow noodles

2 cups finely chopped kale leaves

¼ teaspoon ground turmeric

1 to 2 tablespoons fresh lemon juice

1 cup chopped fresh parsley

Heat the oil in a large pot over medium-low heat. Add the onion, carrots, parsnip, celery, salt, and black pepper and cook for 10 minutes, or until softened. Stir in the garlic, then add the broth, thyme, sage, tomato paste, and chickpeas and simmer over low heat for 20 minutes.

Add the noodles and simmer until the pasta is cooked, about 10 minutes more. Add the kale and cook until just wilted, about 1 minute. Remove the thyme bundle and stir in the turmeric, 1 tablespoon lemon juice, and the parsley. Season to taste with up to ½ teaspoon additional sea salt and up to 1 tablespoon lemon juice, as desired, and serve.

SERVES 6 TO 8

VEGAN & GLUTEN-FREE

TOMATILLO ZUCCHINI WHITE BEAN CHILI

I've always loved tomatoes. At one point, I'd say that they were my absolute favorite food. I loved them raw; sliced; and as marinara, ketchup, tomato salsa, tomato soup, and more. This was all before I moved to Austin, where I discovered my one true love: the tangy tomatillo. I mean, I also discovered Jack in Austin, so I suppose I have two true loves. This chili features the greener of my true loves and is a loose riff on posole. Roasted tomatillos marry with ground-up pepitas, zucchini, jalapeños, and white beans to create this thick, bright vegetarian stew.

⅓ cup pepitas

4 or 5 medium tomatillos, husks removed, rinsed (10 ounces)

1 medium yellow onion, sliced into wedges

1 jalapeño pepper

1 poblano pepper

3 garlic cloves, unpeeled

½ cup fresh cilantro

½ teaspoon sea salt, plus more as needed

Freshly ground black pepper

1 to 2 cups Vegetable Broth (page 104)

1 tablespoon extra-virgin olive oil, plus more for drizzling

2 medium zucchini, diced (3 cups)

1½ cups cooked cannellini beans, drained and rinsed (page 23)

1½ cups cooked chickpeas, drained and rinsed (page 23)

½ teaspoon ground cumin

½ teaspoon ground coriander

1 teaspoon dried oregano

1 cup corn kernels, fresh or frozen

1 tablespoon rice vinegar, plus more as needed

Juice of 1 lime

Topping Options

Sliced jalapeños

Diced avocado

Lime slices

Thinly sliced radish

recipe continues

Place the pepitas in a blender and pulse until blended into a fine powder. Leave the powder in the blender.

Preheat the oven to 450°F and line a large baking sheet with parchment paper. Place the tomatillos, onion wedges, jalapeño, poblano, and garlic cloves on the baking sheet. Drizzle with olive oil and add pinches of salt and pepper and toss to coat. Roast for 25 minutes or until the vegetables are soft and golden brown around the edges. Remove and discard the stems from the peppers and the peel from the garlic. Add the peppers and garlic to the blender, along with the tomatillos, onion, ¼ cup of the cilantro, the sea salt, and 1 cup of the vegetable broth and process until smooth.

Heat the olive oil in a large pot over medium heat. Add the zucchini and a few pinches of salt and pepper and cook until lightly browned, about 3 minutes. Stir in the beans, chickpeas, cumin, coriander, and oregano and cook for 1 minute. Stir in the blended tomatillo mixture, corn kernels, and rice vinegar. Bring to a simmer and cook until warmed through and thickened, about 10 minutes. If the chili is too thick, add 1 more cup of broth. Add the lime juice and season to taste. If you need to temper the spice, add more rice vinegar and/or lime juice, 1 tablespoon at a time, to lessen the proportion of the spice to your taste.

Serve hot with the remaining ¼ cup cilantro and your choice of toppings.

SERVES 4

VEGAN & GLUTEN-FREE

TIP   Store any leftovers in the freezer. You'll thank yourself later.

VERSATILE VEGETABLE LENTIL SOUP

When you have all kinds of leftover vegetable bits and bobs, it's time to make this soup! Have some leeks and half an onion? No carrots but you have sweet potato? Use this recipe as a template to help use up what you have on hand. Serve your creation with crusty bread.

2 tablespoons extra-virgin olive oil

1 medium yellow onion, chopped, or 1½ cups chopped leeks

2 celery stalks or 1 fennel bulb, diced

2 cups diced butternut squash, carrots, or sweet potato

6 kale leaves, stems finely diced, leaves chopped

1 teaspoon sea salt

Freshly ground black pepper

1 cup chopped green beans or 1 small zucchini, diced

3 garlic cloves, minced

Heaping ½ teaspoon ground cumin

2 tablespoons white wine vinegar

1 (14-ounce) can diced fire-roasted tomatoes

6 cups Vegetable Broth (page 104)

12 fresh thyme sprigs, bundled, or 1 tablespoon minced rosemary

¾ cup uncooked French green lentils

Red pepper flakes

½ cup chopped fresh parsley, for garnish

Heat the olive oil in a large pot over medium heat. Add the onion, celery, butternut squash, kale stems, salt, and a few grinds of black pepper. Cook until the vegetables start to soften, about 8 minutes.

Stir in the green beans, garlic, and cumin, followed by the vinegar, tomatoes, broth, thyme, and lentils. Reduce the heat and simmer for 30 minutes, or until the lentils and vegetables are tender. If the stew is too thick, stir in 1 cup water.

Add the kale leaves and cook for 5 minutes more or until wilted. Add a pinch of red pepper flakes and season to taste with salt and pepper. Garnish with the parsley.

SERVES 6

VEGAN & GLUTEN-FREE

Homemade
VEGETABLE BROTH

Place all the ingredients in a large pot and bring to a boil. Reduce the heat and simmer gently, covered, for 1 hour.

Strain and discard the vegetables. Season to taste.

MAKE 8 CUPS

OTHER VEGETABLES TO SWAP IN:

Parsnips, mushrooms, peppers, corn cobs, spring onions, scallions, leeks, ramps, garlic scapes, fresh herbs and their stems.

INGREDIENTS

- **A** 2 medium or 3 small onions, halved
- **B** 4 medium carrots, chopped
- **C** 4 medium celery stalks, chopped
- **D** Fennel or leek tops, chopped
- **E** 1 garlic bulb, halved
- **F** Handful of fresh parsley
- **G** 1 small bunch fresh thyme
- **H** 3 bay leaves
- **I** 2 teaspoons sea salt
- **J** 1 teaspoon black peppercorns
- **K** 12 cups filtered water (3 quarts)

SCRAP STOCK

Simmer the scraps that you might otherwise toss to make a
flavorful broth to add to your favorite soups and stews.

6 loose-packed cups chopped
vegetable scraps

2 teaspoons sea salt

1 teaspoon peppercorns

12 cups water

2 corn cobs with the kernels
cut off (optional)

Place all the ingredients in a
large pot and bring to a boil.
Reduce the heat and simmer gently,
covered, for 1 hour.

Strain and discard the
vegetables. Season to taste.

MAKE 8 CUPS

**Scraps can be
stored in the
freezer until you
have enough to
make stock.**

SAL

ADS

GRILLED ROMAINE VEGAN CAESAR WEDGES

How do you make lettuce exciting? Well, *let us* tell you—grill it! The texture of grilled lettuce goes perfectly with this rich, tangy, versatile, Caesar-like dressing. If you don't have an outdoor grill, this can just as easily be made on a cast-iron grill pan over the stove. If you have extra dressing, flip to page 215 and use it to make the creamy Fennel Fettuccine!

2 slices whole-grain bread

½ garlic clove

Extra-virgin olive oil, for drizzling

3 heads romaine lettuce

2 radishes, sliced paper-thin

2 tablespoons chopped chives

2 teaspoons capers, drained

2 tablespoons hemp seeds

Sea salt and freshly ground black pepper

Lemon wedges, for serving

¼ cup microgreens (optional)

Pinches of red pepper flakes (optional)

Dressing

½ cup raw cashews

1 garlic clove

2 tablespoons fresh lemon juice

2 teaspoons Dijon mustard

2 teaspoons capers, drained

½ cup water

Freshly ground black pepper

Preheat the oven to 350°F. Rub the bread slices with the cut side of the garlic clove and slice the bread into cubes. Toss the bread cubes with a drizzle of olive oil and bake until crispy, 10 to 15 minutes.

Make the dressing: In a high-speed blender, place the cashews, garlic, lemon juice, mustard, capers, water, and a few grinds of black pepper. Blend until creamy.

Preheat a grill or grill pan to high. Slice the romaine heads in half lengthwise, then drizzle with a bit of olive oil and pinches of salt and pepper. Grill the romaine, cut-side down, until char marks form, 1 to 2 minutes. Gently flip the romaine and grill for 2 minutes more.

Assemble the salads with the grilled romaine and a drizzle of the dressing. Top with the radishes, chives, capers, and croutons. Sprinkle with the hemp seeds, microgreens, and red pepper flakes, if using. Serve with the lemon wedges and the remaining dressing on the side.

SERVES 6 | VEGAN | GLUTEN-FREE: Use gluten-free bread or skip the croutons.

SESAME-GINGER AVOCADO FENNEL SALAD

This salad is magic. When I serve it to family and friends, they devour the whole platter. Creamy avocado contrasts with crisp veggies to fill every bite with softness and crunch. The creamy sesame-ginger dressing packs a punch, making this a favorite that comes together in minutes!

Dressing (makes extra)

2½ tablespoons tahini

2 tablespoons fresh lemon juice

2 tablespoons maple syrup

1½ tablespoons tamari

1 tablespoon extra-virgin olive oil

1 tablespoon minced ginger

½ tablespoon sesame oil

1 garlic clove

1 tablespoon water, if needed

Salad

1 fennel bulb, sliced paper-thin

2 carrots, sliced paper-thin

3 red radishes, sliced paper-thin

1 lemon wedge, for squeezing

Sea salt

2 avocados, pitted and thinly sliced

1 tablespoon sesame seeds

¼ cup microgreens

Make the dressing: In a blender, place the tahini, lemon juice, maple syrup, tamari, olive oil, ginger, sesame oil, and garlic and process until smooth. If it's too thick, add the water and blend to a drizzleable consistency.

In a medium bowl, combine the fennel, carrots, and radishes and toss with a large squeeze of lemon and pinches of salt. Spread the fennel mixture on a serving platter and top with the avocado slices. Drizzle generously with the dressing. Sprinkle with the sesame seeds, microgreens, and a few pinches of sea salt to taste. Serve immediately.

SERVES 4 AS A SIDE   VEGAN & GLUTEN-FREE

TIP If you have leftover dressing, drizzle it over a grain bowl the next day. It goes especially well with brown rice and roasted or raw veggies.

PEACH & POLE BEAN SALAD WITH DILL

I have a simple goal every summer, and that is to eat all the peaches. Peach season is fleeting, which is probably why I'm so enamored with them. I love pairing basil with peaches, but once I discovered *dill* with peaches, well, I had yet another reason to love peaches.

2 large handfuls of pole beans, yellow and/or green, trimmed

1 tablespoon extra-virgin olive oil, plus more for drizzling

2 tablespoons fresh lemon juice, plus more to taste

1 large garlic clove, minced

¼ teaspoon Dijon mustard

¼ teaspoon sea salt, plus more to taste

Freshly ground black pepper

1½ cups cooked chickpeas, drained and rinsed (page 23)

1 cup halved cherry tomatoes

¼ cup chopped fresh dill

3 peaches, pitted and sliced

¼ cup sliced almonds, toasted and salted

Prepare a large pot of salted boiling water and a large bowl of ice water. Drop the pole beans into the boiling water and blanch for 2 minutes. Remove the beans and immediately immerse in the ice water to stop the cooking process. Allow the beans to cool completely in the ice water, at least 30 seconds. Drain and place on a kitchen towel to dry.

In a large bowl, combine the olive oil, lemon juice, garlic, mustard, salt, and a few grinds of black pepper.

Add the beans, chickpeas, tomatoes, and half the dill and toss. Just before serving, toss in the peaches, the remaining dill, and a squeeze of lemon juice, as desired. Drizzle with more olive oil and top with the toasted almonds. Season to taste with more salt and pepper and serve.

SERVES 4

VEGAN & GLUTEN-FREE

TIP This is one of my favorite lunch salads—it keeps well in the fridge for up to 3 days.

SOBA SUCCESS

Soba noodles have a tendency to clump more than regular pasta noodles because they are buckwheat-based. There's nothing sadder than soggy soba! To cook perfect soba every time, use this method, which works for soba noodles that are partially made of buckwheat as well as 100 percent buckwheat noodles:

1. Bring a large pot of **unsalted** water to a boil.

2. Cook according to the time listed on the package, or until al dente.

3. Drain into a colander and rinse under cool water to remove the starches that would otherwise make your soba clump.

4. Toss the noodles with a drizzle of sesame oil to keep them from sticking together.

SOBA NOODLE PICNIC SALAD WITH TAHINI MISO

Now that we live in Chicago, when the weather gets nice, we get outside. If there's any consolation prize for surviving a long winter, it's that you learn to really appreciate a nice day. Nice days deserve nice picnic salads like this one.

8 ounces soba noodles

Sesame oil, for drizzling

½ red cabbage, thinly sliced (4 cups)

3 cups loosely packed, finely chopped curly kale

1 cup spiralized or thinly sliced English cucumber

2 carrots, sliced paper-thin (¾ cup)

3 scallions, sliced

Dressing

¼ cup rice vinegar

¼ cup tahini

¼ cup water

2 tablespoons miso paste

2 tablespoons tamari

1 teaspoon sesame oil

½ teaspoon minced ginger

Note: *I usually like to massage raw kale to make it tender enough for raw kale salads. However, chopping it finely achieves a similar goal and is a time saver in this recipe.*

Bring a large pot of water to a boil. Prepare the noodles according to the instructions on the package. Drain and rinse under cold water, running your fingers through them to separate them. Toss with a drizzle of sesame oil.

Make the dressing: In a small bowl, whisk together the rice vinegar, tahini, water, miso paste, tamari, sesame oil, and ginger.

In a medium bowl, toss the cabbage with a few spoonfuls of the dressing.

Divide the remaining dressing among 4 (16-ounce) jars. Layer with the cabbage, kale, cucumber, soba noodles, carrots, and scallions. When ready to eat, pour the salad into a bowl so that the dressing drizzles out on top of the salad, using a spoon or spatula to scoop any that might stick to the bottom of the jar. If serving immediately, assemble the salad in bowls and drizzle the dressing on top.

SERVES 4 | VEGAN | GLUTEN-FREE: Use 100 percent buckwheat soba.

CHIMICHURRI POTATO SALAD

Jack and I went to Argentina for our honeymoon, where I ate a lot of potatoes (sometimes the only vegetable option at dinner) and a lot of chimichurri. Later it dawned on me that those two things, like Jack and me, would actually be wonderful together. This chimichurri is bright, tangy, smoky from the smoked paprika, and a bit spicy. Crisp green beans and radishes round out this veggie-forward potato salad.

2 pounds small potatoes, halved

1 teaspoon sea salt, plus more to taste

12 ounces fresh green beans, trimmed and chopped into 1-inch pieces

3 scallions, finely sliced

Freshly ground black pepper

3 red radishes or 1 watermelon radish, sliced paper-thin

2 cups packed arugula

1½ tablespoons fresh lemon juice

Chimichurri

¼ cup extra-virgin olive oil

¼ cup white wine vinegar

2 small garlic cloves, minced

½ teaspoon red pepper flakes

¼ teaspoon smoked paprika

½ teaspoon sea salt

½ cup finely chopped fresh parsley, 1 tablespoon reserved for garnish

¼ teaspoon dried oregano

Place the potatoes in a large pot and cover with cold water by about 1 inch. Stir in the salt. Bring to a boil, then reduce the heat and simmer, uncovered, until fork-tender, 10 to 14 minutes. Drain the potatoes and set aside to cool to room temperature.

Meanwhile, refill the pot with water, bring it to a boil, and set a bowl of ice water nearby. Drop the green beans into the boiling water and blanch for 2 minutes, drain, and immediately immerse in the ice water to stop the cooking process. After 1 minute, drain and place on a kitchen towel to dry.

Make the chimichurri: In a small bowl, combine the olive oil, vinegar, garlic, red pepper flakes, paprika, salt, parsley, and oregano. This chimichurri might taste sharp on its own, but the flavor will balance as it covers the potatoes in the salad.

Transfer the potatoes to a large mixing bowl. Add the green beans, scallions, three-quarters of the chimichurri, and a few generous pinches of salt and pepper. Gently toss. Mix in the radishes, arugula, lemon juice, and remaining chimichurri. Season with more salt and pepper to taste. Garnish with the reserved 1 tablespoon parsley.

SERVES 6 AS A SIDE

VEGAN & GLUTEN-FREE

oh yeah... Morocco ♡

MOROCCAN-SPICED CARROT SALAD WITH LENTILS

When we visited Morocco, my favorite dish was the traditional carrot salad. I loved the rich spices that made up such a simple, light dish. This version is anything but traditional, but the combination of cumin, coriander, and carrots takes me back to a steamy summer night on the rooftop of the riad where we were staying. Here I combine roasted and raw carrots with lentils, a tangy dressing, and mint. This salad is great for lunch leftovers throughout the week.

---

1 cup dry French green lentils, rinsed

8 medium rainbow carrots (6 chopped into ½-inch pieces, 2 sliced paper-thin)

3 tablespoons extra-virgin olive oil, plus more for drizzling

1 teaspoon sea salt, plus more for sprinkling

Freshly ground black pepper

2 tablespoons apple cider vinegar

1 garlic clove, minced

1 teaspoon grated fresh ginger

1 teaspoon ground cumin

1 teaspoon ground coriander

¼ cup pepitas, toasted and salted

4 cups mixed arugula and baby spinach

½ cup fresh mint leaves

2 teaspoons fresh lemon juice

½ cup Pickled Red Onions (page 297, optional)

Preheat the oven to 425°F and line a baking sheet with parchment paper.

Bring a medium pot of water to a boil, add the lentils, and cook for 15 to 20 minutes, or until tender yet al dente. Drain and rinse under cold water. Shake out the excess water and allow to drain further before adding the lentils to the salad.

Spread the chopped carrots on the baking sheet, drizzle with olive oil, and sprinkle with salt and pepper. Roast for 20 to 25 minutes, or until tender and browned but not mushy.

While the carrots roast, in a large bowl, whisk together the olive oil, apple cider vinegar, garlic, ginger, ½ teaspoon of the cumin, ½ teaspoon of the coriander, the salt, and a few grinds of black pepper. Add the lentils, sliced raw carrots, pepitas, salad greens, mint, and lemon juice to the bowl.

Remove the carrots from the oven, and while they are still warm, toss them with the remaining ½ teaspoon of cumin and coriander. Add them to the salad bowl and toss to combine. Top with the pickled red onions, if using. Season to taste and serve.

SERVES 4

VEGAN & GLUTEN-FREE

TIP   This is also delicious with a sprinkle of feta cheese.

121

SWEET CORN & BLUEBERRY ARUGULA SALAD

I call this the Michigan Summer Salad. My mom drives to Michigan almost every Sunday throughout the summer to spend time at the beach. Once blueberries are in season, she comes home with cases full of them. With a ton of blueberries to use up, I started making this salad with crisp, fresh summer corn. I recommend holding on to this recipe until you have peak-season produce—it's worth the wait.

Dressing

2 tablespoons extra-virgin olive oil

1 tablespoon fresh lemon juice

½ teaspoon Dijon mustard

1 small garlic clove, minced

2 tablespoons finely chopped chives

⅛ teaspoon sea salt

Salad

Kernels from 3 ears of corn

2 scallions, sliced

¼ cup Pickled Red Onions (page 297)

1 cup fresh blueberries

2 peaches, pitted and thinly sliced

2 cups arugula

¼ teaspoon sea salt, plus more to taste

Freshly ground black pepper

1 cup microgreens (optional)

Make the dressing: In a small bowl, whisk together the olive oil, lemon juice, mustard, garlic, chives, and salt. Set aside.

In a large bowl, combine the corn, scallions, pickled onions, blueberries, peaches, and arugula. Drizzle the dressing over the salad and toss. Season with the salt and a few grinds of black pepper. Taste and adjust the seasonings. Garnish with the microgreens, if using.

SERVES 4

VEGAN & GLUTEN-FREE

TIP Make this a lunch salad by storing the tomato-onion-cucumber mixture separately from the toasted pita, yogurt, and chickpeas. Combine when you're ready to eat. Repeat the next day.

HEIRLOOM TOMATO FATTOUSH

This salad is perfect for those who say they don't like salad. Tomatoes, cucumbers, and red onions are marinated in tangy sherry vinegar and a good bit of olive oil. The "dressing" is a layer of lemony yogurt, and the whole thing is topped with crispy pita pieces, roasted spiced chickpeas, and pops of fresh mint. Top with flaky sea salt or a drizzle of tahini, and enjoy this on a warm summer night.

2 whole wheat pitas, sliced into 1-inch pieces (2 cups)

½ cup cooked chickpeas, drained and rinsed (page 23)

2 tablespoons extra-virgin olive oil, plus more for drizzling

½ teaspoon sea salt, plus more for sprinkling

Freshly ground black pepper

¼ teaspoon sumac or sweet paprika

1 tablespoon plus 1 teaspoon fresh lemon juice

1 tablespoon sherry vinegar

1 garlic clove, minced

¼ cup thinly sliced red onion

½ English cucumber, chopped into ½-inch pieces (1½ cups)

3 heirloom tomatoes, sliced into 1-inch wedges (4 cups)

½ cup whole milk Greek yogurt

½ cup chopped fresh mint leaves

Pinches of red pepper flakes

Tahini, for drizzling (optional)

Preheat the oven to 400°F and line 2 baking sheets with parchment paper. Place the pita and the chickpeas on separate baking sheets, and toss each with a drizzle of olive oil and pinches of salt and pepper. Bake the pita until toasted, about 8 minutes. Roast the chickpeas until golden brown and crispy, about 20 minutes. When the chickpeas are out of the oven, toss with the sumac or sweet paprika. Set aside.

In the bottom of a medium bowl, combine the olive oil, 1 tablespoon of the lemon juice, the sherry vinegar, garlic, and ¼ teaspoon of the sea salt. Add the red onion and toss to coat. Add the cucumber, tomatoes, another sprinkle of salt, and a few grinds of black pepper. Toss and set aside for 5 minutes.

In a small bowl, combine the yogurt with the remaining 1 teaspoon lemon juice and ¼ teaspoon sea salt.

Assemble the salad by spreading the yogurt on the bottom of a serving dish. Pile on the tomato-cucumber mixture, leaving behind some of the juices if it seems too watery, then add the pita, chickpeas, fresh mint, and a drizzle of olive oil. Add the red pepper flakes and season to taste.

Top with a drizzle of tahini, if desired. If your tahini is too thick, add a bit of water to thin.

SERVES 4

VEGAN: Skip the yogurt and drizzle ¼ cup Lemon Tahini Dressing (page 130) on top of the salad.

TIP Keep the leftover beet greens for another meal— see page 24 for ideas!

BEET SALAD WITH PISTACHIO BEET GREEN GREMOLATA

Beet greens are the best! If you gain one tip from this book, it's that you should use the tops of beets when they're fresh and lush. Unlike some bitter greens, beet tops are wonderfully mild and lightly sweet. Instead of chopping up herbs to use in this gremolata, I chopped up the beet greens. While grapefruit may seem like an odd pairing, its bright acidity complements the other flavors in this pink on pink on pink salad.

❖

1 bunch beets with greens attached (5 small/medium)

Extra-virgin olive oil, for drizzling

Sea salt and freshly ground black pepper

1 cup chopped radicchio or 2 endive spears, chopped

2 radishes or 1 scarlet turnip, sliced paper-thin

1 grapefruit, segments cut out, plus its juices squeezed from the membranes

Sherry vinegar, for drizzling

Pickled Red Onions (page 297, optional)

¼ cup microgreens (optional)

Pistachio Beet Green Gremolata

2 tablespoons fresh lemon juice

1 teaspoon lemon zest

1 garlic clove, minced

1½ cups finely minced beet greens

¼ cup crushed pistachios

Sea salt and freshly ground black pepper

2 tablespoons extra-virgin olive oil

Preheat the oven to 425°F. Clip the beets from their greens and set the greens aside.

Wrap the beets in aluminum foil with a drizzle of olive oil and a pinch of salt. Roast for 60 minutes or until fork-tender. The timing will depend on the size and freshness of the beets. Remove the roasted beets from the oven and unwrap the foil. When they are cool to the touch, hold the beets under running water and use your hands to slide off the skins. Slice the beets into wedges and chill until ready to use.

Make the beet green gremolata: In a medium bowl, combine the lemon juice, lemon zest, and garlic. Stir in the minced beet greens, pistachios, and a generous pinch of salt and pepper. Stir in the olive oil and season to taste.

Assemble the radicchio and radishes on a serving platter and drizzle with olive oil, grapefruit juice, and pinches of salt and pepper. Toss gently. Add the grapefruit segments and beets, and drizzle with sherry vinegar, more grapefruit juice, and more olive oil. Top with the pickled red onions, if using, and spoonfuls of the beet green gremolata. Sprinkle with the microgreens, if desired, and pinches of salt.

SERVES 4 AS A SIDE

VEGAN & GLUTEN-FREE

GEM SALAD WITH CREAMY DILL DRESSING

This salad is spring in a bowl. With blanched asparagus, peas, radishes, and fresh herbs dolloped with creamy dill dressing, it's a great way to use your early farmers market veggies.

Creamy Dill Dressing (makes extra)

1 ripe avocado

3 tablespoons fresh lemon juice

½ garlic clove

¼ cup roughly chopped fresh dill, plus more for garnish

½ cup water, plus more as needed

½ teaspoon sea salt

Freshly ground black pepper

Salad

2 slices whole-grain bread, cubed

Extra-virgin olive oil, for drizzling

Flaky sea salt, for sprinkling

6 ounces asparagus, tender parts, chopped into 1-inch pieces

3 ounces gem or butterhead lettuce

¼ cup peas, thawed if frozen, blanched if fresh

1 watermelon radish or 2 red radishes, sliced paper-thin

2 Persian cucumbers, peeled into ribbons

¼ cup Pickled Red Onions (page 297)

½ ripe avocado, diced

2 tablespoons fresh mint leaves

2 tablespoons minced chives

¼ cup crumbled feta cheese

Preheat the oven to 350°F and line a baking sheet with parchment paper.

Make the creamy dill dressing: In a blender, place the avocado, lemon juice, garlic, dill, water, salt, and a few grinds of pepper and blend until smooth. If the dressing is too thick, add a bit more water or olive oil, as desired.

Toss the bread cubes with a drizzle of olive oil and a pinch of flaky sea salt and bake until crispy, 10 to 15 minutes.

Bring a large pot of salted water to a boil and set a bowl of ice water nearby. Drop the asparagus into the boiling water and blanch for 1 to 2 minutes, until tender but still bright green. Use a slotted spoon to scoop the asparagus out of the boiling water and into the ice water. Chill for 1 minute, then drain and transfer to a kitchen towel to dry.

To assemble the salad, place the gem lettuce on a platter and top with a few evenly spaced dollops of the dressing. Scatter on the asparagus, peas, croutons, radish, cucumbers, pickled red onions, avocado, mint, chives, and feta cheese. Top with more dill and more dollops of the dressing. Sprinkle generously with flaky sea salt and serve.

SERVES 4 TO 6

TIP Spread leftover dressing on toast the next day.

SALAD DRESSINGS

{ SEASON WITH SEA SALT AND FRESHLY GROUND BLACK PEPPER TO TASTE }

LEMON THYME	2 tablespoons lemon juice	1 garlic clove, minced	½ teaspoon Dijon mustard	2 teaspoons thyme leaves	¼ cup olive oil	+ ¼ teaspoon sea salt
LEMON LEMONGRASS	½ cup coconut milk	2 teaspoons minced lemongrass	2 teaspoons lemon juice	1 teaspoon tamari	1 teaspoon grated ginger	+ ¼ teaspoon sea salt
MEDITERRANEAN	1 tablespoon sherry vinegar	1 garlic clove, minced	½ teaspoon dried oregano	1 diced sun-dried tomato	¼ cup olive oil	+ ¼ teaspoon sea salt
LEMON TAHINI	¼ cup tahini	2 tablespoons lemon juice	3 tablespoons water	1 garlic clove, minced	½ teaspoon maple syrup	+ ¼ teaspoon sea salt
SESAME ORANGE	¼ cup fresh orange juice	2 tablespoons rice vinegar	1 tablespoon tamari	½ teaspoon sriracha	1 teaspoon sesame oil	
GINGER MISO	2 tablespoons miso	2 tablespoons rice vinegar	1 tablespoon tamari	1 teaspoon minced ginger	2 tablespoons olive oil	
CASHEW COCONUT	¼ cup cashew butter	½ cup coconut milk	2 tablespoons lime juice	1 tablespoon tamari	1 teaspoon sriracha	

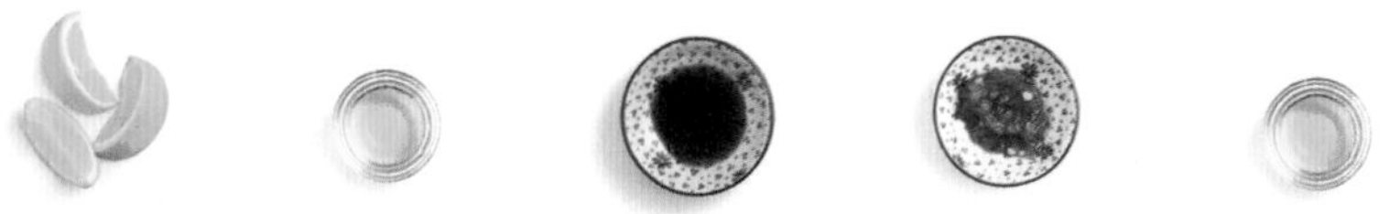

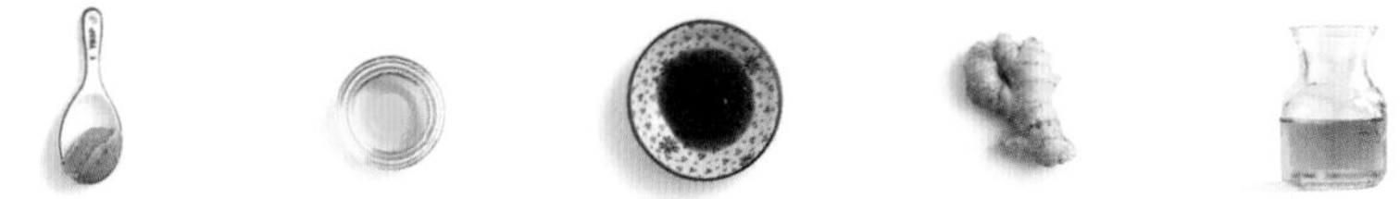

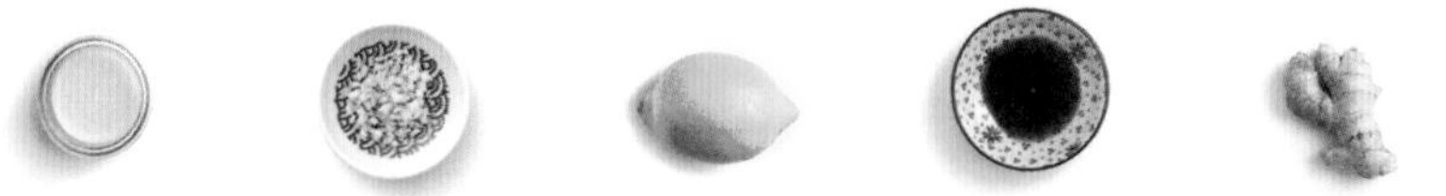

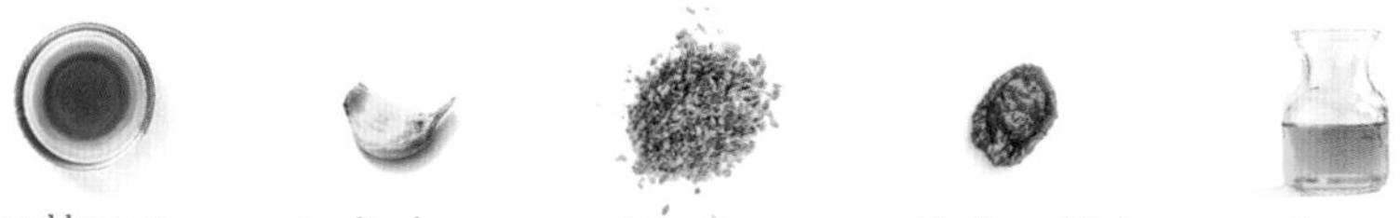

CHICKPEA GODDESS	¼ cup hummus	¼ cup water	1 tablespoon minced parsley	1 tablespoon minced chives	2 teaspoons minced tarragon	+ ¼ teaspoon sea salt
PESTO VINAIGRETTE	¼ cup ground pine nuts	2 tablespoons lemon juice	1 garlic clove, minced	2 tablespoons minced basil	¼ cup olive oil	+ ¼ teaspoon sea salt
CHIPOTLE AIOLI	⅓ cup mayo	2 tablespoons lime juice	1 garlic clove, minced	½ teaspoon maple syrup	1 teaspoon chipotle powder	
CARROT GINGER (BLEND)	½ cup chopped roasted carrots	2 tablespoons rice vinegar	2 teaspoons minced ginger	¼ cup olive oil	½ cup water	+ ¼ teaspoon sea salt
RED PEPPER MOJO (BLEND)	1 roasted red pepper	1 clove roasted garlic	2 tablespoons lime juice	1 teaspoon smoked paprika	¼ cup olive oil	+ ¼ teaspoon sea salt
CURRY YOGURT	½ cup Greek yogurt	1 tablespoon lemon juice	1 tablespoon olive oil	1 teaspoon curry powder	1 tablespoon water	+ ¼ teaspoon sea salt
APPLE CIDER SAGE	¼ cup olive oil	2 tablespoons apple cider vinegar	2 teaspoons maple syrup	½ teaspoon cinnamon	16 sage leaves, chopped	+ ½ teaspoon sea salt
HEALTHIER RANCH (BLEND)	½ cup raw cashews	½ cup water	⅓ cup diced cucumber	2 tablespoons lime juice	½ garlic clove	+ ½ teaspoon sea salt
CREAMY DILL (BLEND)	1 ripe avocado, pitted	3 tablespoons lemon juice	½ garlic clove	¼ cup fresh dill	½ cup water	+ ½ teaspoon sea salt

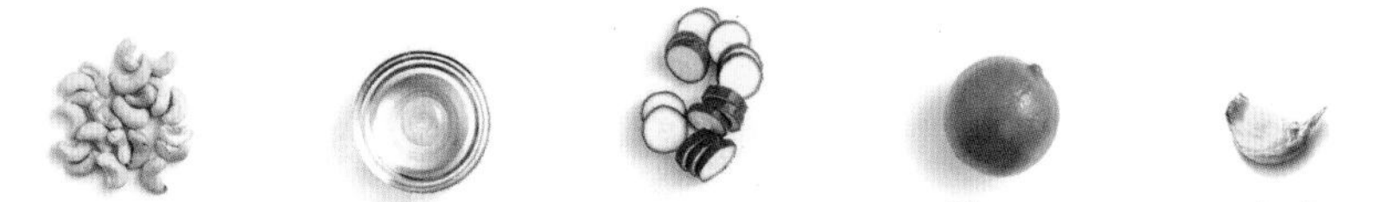

FOR DINNER

CHAPTER

ASPARAGUS, SNAP PEA & CHIVE BLOSSOM PASTA

Our farmers market visits may be weather dependent now that we live in Chicago, but when the season is right, the markets are flourishing. This recipe was inspired by a visit to the Logan Square Farmers Market in the early spring. I came home with some gorgeous snap peas, asparagus, and these perfect purple chive blossoms that are delicious sprinkled over everything (note: regular chives work here too). The pasta shape in this recipe mimics the size of the snap peas and the cut asparagus. It feels like you're eating a big plate of pasta, but really it's half vegetables.

Zest and juice of 1 lemon

1½ teaspoons Dijon mustard

10 ounces penne or casarecce pasta

2 tablespoons extra-virgin olive oil

5 radishes, halved or quartered

1 (8-ounce) bunch asparagus, ends trimmed, cut into 1-inch pieces

1½ cups snap peas, trimmed

⅓ cup chopped chives

½ teaspoon sea salt, plus more to taste

Freshly ground black pepper

2 garlic cloves, minced

¼ cup dry white wine

⅔ cup grated Parmesan cheese

3 tablespoons chive blossoms or chopped chives

2 tablespoons thyme flowers or fresh thyme leaves

Mix together the lemon juice and mustard. Set aside.

Bring a large pot of salted water to a boil. Prepare the pasta according to the instructions on the package, cooking until al dente. Reserve ½ cup of the starchy pasta water, then drain.

Heat 1 tablespoon of the olive oil in a large skillet over medium heat. Add the radishes, asparagus, snap peas, chives, salt, and a few grinds of pepper. Cook for 3 to 4 minutes, until the green vegetables are tender but still have a vibrant bite. Stir in the garlic and the white wine and cook for 1 minute to slightly reduce the wine.

Remove the skillet from the heat and stir in the pasta. Add the lemon-mustard mixture, the reserved pasta water, ⅓ cup of the Parmesan cheese, and the lemon zest. Toss until coated. Taste and adjust seasonings.

Transfer to a platter and garnish with the chive blossoms and the thyme flowers. Drizzle with the remaining 1 tablespoon olive oil and serve with the remaining ⅓ cup Parmesan cheese.

SERVES 4

GLUTEN-FREE: Use gluten-free pasta.

BAKED RED LENTIL FALAFEL

At the risk of over-chickpea-ing this book, I made this falafel recipe out of red lentils. Just a heads-up, the lentils in this recipe need to be soaked overnight. After that, these falafel come together in just a few pulses of the food processor. Drizzle them with a little olive oil before baking so that they become crisp without frying. Just don't taste this mixture before you bake it—the raw lentils are very bitter. Once they come out, though, you'll see why this one is so special.

---

1 cup uncooked red lentils, soaked overnight, drained and rinsed

1 medium shallot, chopped (about ⅓ cup)

¼ cup hemp seeds

3 garlic cloves

1 teaspoon ground cumin

1 teaspoon ground coriander

¼ teaspoon cayenne pepper

1 teaspoon lemon zest

1 teaspoon sea salt

¼ teaspoon baking powder

1 cup chopped fresh cilantro leaves and stems

1 cup chopped fresh parsley leaves and stems

1 tablespoon extra-virgin olive oil, plus more for drizzling

¼ cup panko bread crumbs

Lemon-Tahini Sauce

¼ cup tahini

2 tablespoons fresh lemon juice

3 tablespoons water, plus more as needed

¼ teaspoon sea salt

For Serving

4 (6-inch) whole-grain pitas

1 cup chopped romaine lettuce

½ cup Pickled Red Onions (page 297)

1 cup diced cucumber

1 watermelon radish, sliced paper-thin

¼ cup fresh cilantro or mint leaves

Homemade Harissa (page 281), or store-bought (optional)

recipe continues

Preheat the oven to 425°F and line a large baking sheet with parchment paper.

In a large food processor, place the soaked lentils (they will be plump but still raw at this point), shallot, hemp seeds, garlic, cumin, coriander, cayenne, lemon zest, salt, baking powder, cilantro, parsley, and olive oil. Pulse until well combined but not pureed. Use a spatula to scrape down the sides of the bowl as needed. Transfer to a medium bowl and stir in the panko.

Use a 2-tablespoon scoop to form the falafel mixture into 18 balls (be careful not to pack the balls too tight or your falafel will be dense). Place the balls on the baking sheet and gently press to form thick patties. Drizzle the patties with olive oil and bake for 10 minutes. Flip and bake for 7 minutes more or until golden brown and crisp on the outside. During the last few minutes of baking, wrap the pita in foil and warm in the oven.

Meanwhile, make the lemon-tahini sauce: In a small bowl, whisk together the tahini, lemon juice, water, and salt. Thin with more water as needed for a drizzleable consistency.

Slice the warm pita pockets in half and stuff each with a drizzle of lemon-tahini sauce, a slather of the harissa, if using, the romaine, some of the pickled onions, 2 or 3 falafel patties, the cucumber, radish, more pickled onions, more tahini sauce, and the cilantro or mint. Serve with the remaining tahini sauce.

SERVES 4 | VEGAN | GLUTEN-FREE: Use gluten-free panko and pita.

COZY VEGAN MUSHROOM & WHITE BEAN POTPIE

Every November, I like to come up with one vegetarian main course recipe to post on our blog for Thanksgiving. A vegan potpie has been on my list for a while, but when this recipe turned out *so* well, I knew I wanted to save it for this book! The hearty mushroom and white bean filling comes together in no time, and the earthiness from the fresh thyme plays perfectly against the tangy balsamic vinegar. The crust here is our vegan crust made with refined coconut oil.

Crust

¾ cup whole wheat pastry flour

¾ cup all-purpose flour, plus more for rolling

1 tablespoon cane sugar

½ teaspoon sea salt

½ cup plus 1 tablespoon refined* coconut oil, solid but still scoopable

3 to 4 tablespoons ice water

*Use refined instead of virgin or unrefined coconut oil to avoid giving the potpies a coconut flavor.

Filling

1 tablespoon cornstarch

1 cup Vegetable Broth (page 104)

1 tablespoon extra-virgin olive oil

1 medium yellow onion, chopped

2 celery stalks, chopped

1 teaspoon sea salt, plus more to taste

16 ounces cremini mushrooms, sliced (4 cups)

2 tablespoons balsamic vinegar

3 cups cooked cannellini beans, drained and rinsed (page 23)

2 garlic cloves, minced

2 tablespoons fresh thyme leaves

Freshly ground black pepper

recipe continues

Make the crust: In a medium bowl, whisk together the flours, sugar, and salt.

Transfer half of the flour mixture to a food processor and scoop in the coconut oil by large separate spoonfuls. Pulse until the mixture starts to become crumbly, 12 to 16 pulses, then add the remaining flour and pulse until the mixture resembles coarse sand, about 8 more pulses.

Transfer the crumbly dough back to the original bowl. Add the ice water, 1 tablespoon at a time, and use a rubber spatula to fold and form the dough until it sticks together in a cohesive ball. Knead the dough a few times to get it to come together in a smooth ball. Form the dough into a 1½-inch-thick disk, wrap it in plastic wrap, and chill for 30 minutes.

Meanwhile, make the filling: In a small bowl, whisk together the cornstarch and ¼ cup of the vegetable broth. Set aside. Heat the olive oil in a large skillet over medium heat. Add the onion, celery, and salt and cook until soft, about 5 minutes. Add the mushrooms and cook, stirring or shaking the pan occasionally, until soft, about 8 minutes. Stir in the balsamic vinegar, then add the beans, garlic, remaining ¾ cup broth, the thyme, and a

few grinds of black pepper. Bring to a high simmer and stir in the cornstarch mixture to thicken the filling. Turn off the heat.

Preheat the oven to 400°F.

Place the chilled dough on a lightly floured surface or on floured parchment paper. Roll the dough into a 7-inch circle, then flip it and dust the surface with a bit more flour before placing the dough back down. Continue to roll the dough until it's ⅛ inch thick. If the dough is too firm, let it sit for 10 minutes at room temperature. If it's too sticky, add more flour. If the dough cracks, patch it and continue rolling. Using your ramekin as a measure, cut out 4 to 6 circles (depending on the size of the ramekin) ½ inch larger all around than the ramekin.

Distribute the filling into 4 (12-ounce) or 6 (8-ounce) ramekins or similar and gently place a dough circle on top. Tuck the overhang under itself and crimp the edges with your fingers.

Place the ramekins on a baking sheet and bake for 25 to 30 minutes, or until the crust is golden brown.

These freeze well. Reheat frozen pies in a 350°F oven for 45 minutes.

SERVES 4 TO 6

VEGAN

TIP If you don't have individual ramekins, this can be baked in a 9-inch pie dish with the crust on top.

CAULIFLOWER STEAKS WITH LEMON SALSA VERDE

Cauliflower is so versatile, and I love how this recipe uses the cauliflower from floret to core. The "steaks" are cut from the middle section, where the core holds the slabs together. The remaining florets are used to make a creamy puree. It's a warm, hearty dish that gets a pop from the bright preserved lemon salsa verde on top.

---

1 medium cauliflower

2 tablespoons extra-virgin olive oil, plus more for drizzling

Sea salt and freshly ground black pepper

2 garlic cloves

1 tablespoon white miso paste

1 tablespoon fresh lemon juice

1 tablespoon water, plus more as needed

Lemon zest, for garnish (optional)

Lemon Salsa Verde

3 tablespoons diced Quick Preserved Lemons (page 279)

¼ cup finely chopped parsley or basil

2 teaspoons capers

2 tablespoons toasted pine nuts

¼ teaspoon red pepper flakes and/or 1 tiny red chile pepper, thinly sliced

Sea salt and freshly ground black pepper

2 tablespoons extra-virgin olive oil

Preheat the oven to 425°F and line a baking sheet with parchment paper.

Remove the coarse outer leaves of the cauliflower, then slice 4 (1-inch-thick) "steaks" from the middle of the cauliflower, keeping the core intact. This helps hold the steaks together. Place the steaks on the baking sheet, drizzle with olive oil, and rub liberally on both sides with salt and pepper. Roast for 30 minutes, or until the core is fork-tender.

Break the remainder of the cauliflower into florets (about 2 cups) and bring a medium pot of salted water to a boil. Add the cauliflower florets and the garlic cloves and cook for 5 to 7 minutes, or until fork-tender. Use a slotted spoon to transfer the florets and garlic to a high-speed blender. Let cool slightly, and then add the olive oil, miso paste, lemon juice, and water. Puree the mixture, using the blender baton to help keep the blade moving or pausing to stir as necessary. If needed, add 1 to 2 tablespoons more water to create a smooth puree. Season to taste.

Make the lemon salsa verde: In a medium bowl, combine the preserved lemons, parsley, capers, pine nuts, red pepper flakes, and pinches of salt and pepper. Stir in the olive oil.

Assemble each plate with a scoop of the cauliflower puree and a cauliflower steak. Top with the lemon salsa verde and garnish with the lemon zest, if desired. Season to taste with more salt and pepper and serve.

SERVES 4

VEGAN & GLUTEN-FREE

SHIITAKE BOK CHOY BUDDHA BOWLS

This is my favorite kind of comfort food. It's warm, it's cozy, and it makes me feel nourished and satisfied but not weighed down. The creamy walnut sauce pulls it all together—it's so good, you're going to want to pour it on everything!

Sriracha Tofu

14 ounces extra-firm tofu, patted dry and cubed

2 tablespoons tamari, plus more for drizzling

½ teaspoon sriracha, plus more for serving

Walnut-Ginger Miso Sauce (makes extra)

½ cup walnuts

2 tablespoons rice vinegar

2 tablespoons white miso paste

½-inch piece of fresh ginger, minced

½ garlic clove

½ teaspoon maple syrup

¼ to ⅓ cup water

For the Bowls

2 teaspoons extra-virgin olive oil, plus more for drizzling

10 ounces shiitake mushrooms, stemmed and sliced

1 teaspoon rice vinegar

1 bunch of greens, large leaves chopped (tatsoi, chard, bok choy, or kale)

2 cups cooked brown rice (page 22)

2 tablespoons thinly sliced pickled ginger

½ cup microgreens

1 tablespoon sesame seeds

Make the sriracha tofu: Preheat the oven to 425°F and line a baking sheet with parchment paper. Toss the tofu with the tamari and spread evenly onto the baking sheet. Bake for 20 minutes. Remove from the oven and toss with the sriracha.

Make the sauce: In a blender, place the walnuts, rice vinegar, miso paste, fresh ginger, garlic, maple syrup, and ¼ cup of water and process until smooth. Add more water as needed to blend to a smooth consistency.

Make the bowl base: Heat the olive oil in a medium skillet over medium heat. Add the mushrooms and toss to coat. Cook, stirring only occasionally, until the mushrooms are wilted and soft. Add a drizzle of tamari and shake the pan to coat the mushrooms. Add the rice vinegar, stir, then transfer to a plate and set aside.

Wipe out the pan and fill with ½ inch of water. Add the greens, cover, and let them steam until wilted and tender but still bright green, 3 to 6 minutes depending on the type of greens you are using. Remove from the pan and drain any excess water.

Toss the brown rice with a little bit of the miso sauce and assemble bowls with the rice, greens, mushrooms, tofu, pickled ginger, microgreens, and sesame seeds. Serve with the remaining walnut-ginger miso sauce, tamari, and sriracha on the side.

SERVES 4

VEGAN & GLUTEN-FREE

BROCCOLI RICE BLACK BEAN BURRITOS

I've been ricing cauliflower for years, but the vibrant color of traditional Mexican green rice got me thinking—what about broccoli rice? This light burrito filling uses the whole broccoli head—from stem to floret—and with a little brown rice stirred in for texture and a punch of flavor from cilantro and lime, it's made me a broccoli rice convert! I love this as an actual burrito, but if you're more of a burrito bowl person, serve these components all in a bowl! Don't skip the chipotle aioli—it really kicks things up a notch.

Chipotle Aioli

⅓ cup mayonnaise

2 tablespoons fresh lime juice

1 garlic clove, minced

½ teaspoon maple syrup

1 teaspoon chipotle powder*

Quick Pico

1 cup diced tomato (1 to 2 small tomatoes)

½ cup diced white onion

¼ cup chopped fresh cilantro

2 tablespoons fresh lime juice

1 garlic clove, minced

½ jalapeño pepper, stemmed and diced

¼ teaspoon sea salt

This sauce is on the spicy side. If you're sensitive to spice, use ½ teaspoon chipotle powder.

Cilantro-Lime Broccoli Rice

1 small broccoli head with stalk (8 ounces)

Extra-virgin olive oil, for brushing

2 scallions, diced

1 garlic clove, minced

2 tablespoons chopped cilantro stems, plus ½ cup leaves reserved

¼ teaspoon sea salt, plus more to taste

Freshly ground black pepper

¼ teaspoon ground cumin, plus more to taste

1 lime, for squeezing

1 cup cooked brown rice (page 22)

For Serving

4 large flour tortillas

1 cup cooked black beans, drained and rinsed (page 23)

1 ripe avocado, pitted and diced (optional)

⅓ cup crumbled feta or Cotija cheese (optional)

recipe continues

Make the chipotle aioli: In a small bowl, mix together the mayo, lime juice, garlic, maple syrup, and chipotle powder. Chill until ready to use.

Make the quick pico: In a small bowl, combine the tomato, onion, cilantro, lime juice, garlic, jalapeño, and salt. Toss to combine and set aside.

Make the broccoli rice: Remove any tough, woody parts from the broccoli stalks. Chop the remaining stalk and the florets into 1-inch pieces. Place into a food processor and pulse until the broccoli is broken up into tiny rice-sized pieces. This should yield about 2 cups of "riced" broccoli. Heat a nonstick skillet over medium-low heat and brush with olive oil. Add the riced broccoli, the scallions, garlic, cilantro stems, salt, and a few grinds of pepper. Cook and stir for 1 minute, until lightly warmed but still bright green. Remove the pan from the heat and stir in the cumin, a squeeze of lime juice, and the brown rice. Season to taste and set aside.

Prepare the burritos: Slightly warm the tortillas over the flame of a gas stove or in the oven wrapped in foil, so that they're pliable. Load the fillings into the center of the tortillas: the broccoli rice, black beans, avocado, if using, and the quick pico. Drizzle with the chipotle aioli and sprinkle with the reserved cilantro leaves and the crumbled cheese, if using. Roll the burritos, tucking the sides in, and serve.

SERVES 4

VEGAN: Use vegan mayo in the aioli, and skip the cheese.

GLUTEN-FREE: Use gluten-free tortillas.

TIP Save time and use frozen brown rice (page 38) in this recipe. Reheat it in the microwave before using, or let it thaw at room temperature for 30 minutes.

HOW TO RICE VEGETABLES

Cauliflower rice became a huge trend, but you can "rice" other veggies too! Here are my favorites:

Broccoli
Cauliflower
Carrots
Beets

1.

Make sure your vegetable is fully dry.

2.

Chop into 1-inch pieces. For broccoli and cauliflower, be sure to include the stems as well as the florets.

3.

Place the vegetable pieces in a food processor and pulse until they have the texture of rice. Work in batches if necessary, and don't overprocess—that will make your "rice" mushy.

4.

I like to season and cook my "rice" according to the broccoli rice method opposite. Use in any recipe that calls for a side of rice or get creative making your own colorful veggie bowls!

TIP

If you don't have pickled red onion brine handy,
marinate the sliced turnips in white wine vinegar
with a pinch of sea salt and cane sugar.

SPRING-ON-A-PLATE SOCCA FLATBREAD

Socca is a chickpea-based flatbread that we've enjoyed in Nice and in Buenos Aires. It requires just three ingredients and only one funny flour (chickpea flour), but you're going to make this over and over again, so I promise it's worth it. The trick to successful crisp-edged socca is making sure your cast-iron skillet is screaming hot before the batter goes in, so be sure to put the skillet in the oven before preheating.

½ scarlet turnip or 2 red radishes, very thinly sliced

Brine from Pickled Red Onions (page 297)

1 tablespoon extra-virgin olive oil

Sunny Spinach Herb Spread (page 300)

⅓ cup frozen peas, thawed

⅓ cup crumbled feta cheese

1 to 2 tablespoons chopped Quick Preserved Lemons (page 279)

¼ cup fresh mint leaves

¼ teaspoon red pepper flakes

Socca

1 cup chickpea flour

1 cup water

2 tablespoons extra-virgin olive oil

½ teaspoon sea salt

Cut the turnip slices into quarters (if using small red radishes, just leave them as round slices). In a small jar or bowl, combine the sliced turnip with enough brine from the pickled onions to cover. Set aside and let marinate for 1 hour.

Preheat the oven to 475°F with a 12-inch cast-iron skillet inside.

Make the socca: In a medium bowl, combine the chickpea flour, water, olive oil, and salt and whisk until smooth. Cover and set aside to soak for 30 minutes.

Using a pot holder, remove the pre-heated skillet from the oven and add the 1 tablespoon olive oil, brushing to coat the bottom and sides of the pan. Pour the batter into the pan and bake for 17 to 19 minutes, or until the socca is well browned and crisp around the edges. Do not underbake—the crispier the better. Remove from the oven, let cool slightly, and then use a spatula to loosen and transfer the socca from the skillet to a serving plate.

Spread the socca with the spinach herb spread and top with the drained turnip pieces, peas, feta, preserved lemons, mint leaves, and red pepper flakes. Slice into wedges and serve.

SERVES 2   VEGAN: Skip the cheese.   GLUTEN-FREE

BREADED & BAKED ARTICHOKE "FISH" TACOS

This recipe started as a vegetarian riff on a po'boy sandwich. I loved the combination of briny baked artichokes with tangy tartar-like sauce, but I liked the filling so much more than the bread surrounding it. I nixed this recipe, until I thought: taco! A thin flour tortilla lets the filling shine. These tacos also work well with butternut squash, cauliflower, or oyster mushrooms if you want to change up your filling from time to time.

2 cups shredded red cabbage

1 teaspoon extra-virgin olive oil

1 tablespoon fresh lime juice, plus 4 wedges for serving

¼ teaspoon sea salt, plus more to taste

1 serrano pepper, sliced (optional)

Freshly ground black pepper

8 (6-inch) tortillas, warmed or lightly charred

Greek Yogurt Tartar Sauce (page 304)

2 radishes, thinly sliced

½ cup chopped fresh cilantro

Artichokes

1 tablespoon ground flaxseed

¼ cup plus 2 tablespoons almond milk

1 (14-ounce) can whole artichoke hearts

1 cup panko bread crumbs

2 tablespoons hemp seeds

½ teaspoon smoked paprika

¼ teaspoon onion powder

¼ teaspoon sea salt

Freshly ground black pepper

Extra-virgin olive oil, for drizzling

½ lemon, for squeezing

In a medium bowl, toss the red cabbage with the olive oil, lime juice, salt, peppers, if using, and several grinds of black pepper. Set aside.

Prepare the artichokes: Preheat the oven to 425°F and line a baking sheet with parchment paper.

In a small bowl, combine the ground flaxseed with the almond milk and set aside to thicken for 5 minutes.

Drain the artichokes, slice them in half, and then pat dry. In a medium bowl, combine the panko, hemp seeds, smoked paprika, onion powder, salt, and several grinds of pepper.

Dip each artichoke piece in the flaxseed mixture and then the panko mixture. Place onto the baking sheet and drizzle with olive oil. Bake for 20 minutes or until browned and crispy. Remove the artichokes from the oven and sprinkle generously with more salt and pepper and a good squeeze of lemon.

To assemble the tacos, fill the tortillas with the yogurt sauce, cabbage salad, radishes, artichokes (2 or 3 per taco), and fresh cilantro. Serve with lime wedges.

SERVES 4

ZUCCHINI VERDE VEGAN ENCHILADAS

I love enchiladas. I'm tempted to order them at restaurants, but they're often a big cheese bomb on a plate, so I prefer to make them at home. These have no cheese and are packed with a triple threat of green things: zucchini, poblano, and tomatillos. There's tofu in the filling, but it's undetectable once baked in. Instead of cheese on top, a lime cashew cream gets drizzled on along with the other fresh fixings.

— ◆◆ —

Cashew Lime Sour Cream

1 cup raw cashews

1 cup water

1 garlic clove

2 tablespoons fresh lime juice

Heaping ¼ teaspoon sea salt

Enchiladas

1 tablespoon extra-virgin olive oil, plus more for brushing

1 small yellow onion, halved and thinly sliced

1 poblano pepper, stemmed and seeded, sliced into thin strips

½ teaspoon sea salt, plus more to taste

1 small zucchini, halved lengthwise, then cut into thin half-moons

½ teaspoon ground coriander

½ teaspoon ground cumin

2 garlic cloves, minced

½ teaspoon freshly ground black pepper

1 cup cooked black beans, drained and rinsed (page 23)

6 ounces firm tofu, patted dry and crumbled

1½ cups Tomatillo Salsa (page 287), or store-bought

8 corn tortillas, warmed*

Toppings

¼ cup diced red onion

2 radishes, sliced paper-thin

½ avocado, diced

½ cup chopped fresh cilantro

½ jalapeño or serrano pepper, thinly sliced (optional)

Lime slices, for serving

Warm the tortillas for 20 seconds in the microwave, wrapped in damp paper towels, or heat for 10 minutes in the oven, wrapped in aluminum foil.

recipe continues

Preheat the oven to 400°F.

Make the cashew lime sour cream: In a high-speed blender, place the cashews, water, garlic, lime juice, and salt and blend until smooth. Chill until ready to use.

Make the enchilada filling: In a large skillet, heat the olive oil over medium heat. Add the onion, poblano, and a pinch of salt and cook until the onion is soft, about 5 minutes. Add the zucchini, coriander, and cumin and cook until lightly browned, about 5 minutes more.

Stir in the garlic, salt, and black pepper. Remove from the heat and transfer to a large bowl. Stir in the black beans and tofu.

Brush a 9×13-inch baking dish with olive oil, then spread a heaping ½ cup of the tomatillo salsa on the bottom of the dish. Fill each tortilla with about ½ cup of the enchilada filling. Roll the tortillas and place them seam-side down in the baking dish. Pour the remaining 1 cup salsa over the enchiladas, down the middle, leaving a bit of the edges dry. I do this so that the edges of the tortillas become a little crunchy. Bake, covered, for 15 minutes. Uncover and bake for 10 minutes more.

Let the enchiladas cool slightly, then drizzle with half of the cashew lime sour cream. Top with the diced red onion, radishes, avocado, cilantro, and jalapeño, if using. Serve with the lime slices and remaining cashew cream on the side.

SERVES 4   VEGAN & GLUTEN-FREE

RADISH "NOODLES" WITH CASHEW-COCONUT SAUCE

This is the recipe to make if you're like me and you love picking up pretty, colorful radishes at the farmers market and figuring out what to do with them later! Now you can take any bunch of lovely radishes, noodle them, and add tofu, fresh herbs, and this spicy cashew-coconut sauce.

7 ounces extra-firm tofu, patted dry and cubed

1 tablespoon tamari

4 ounces kelp noodles or vermicelli rice noodles

¼ cup crushed cashews

1 teaspoon extra-virgin olive oil

2 scallions, sliced into ½-inch pieces

1 large daikon radish, spiralized (7 ounces)

1 purple daikon or watermelon radish, spiralized

1 large carrot, spiralized

1 English cucumber, spiralized

½ cup bean sprouts

½ cup chopped fresh cilantro

Lime wedges, for serving

Red pepper flakes (optional)

Cashew-Coconut Sauce

¼ cup cashew butter

½ cup full-fat coconut milk

2 tablespoons lime juice

1 tablespoon tamari, plus more for serving

1 teaspoon sriracha, plus more for serving

Preheat the oven to 425°F and line a baking sheet with parchment paper. Toss the tofu with the tamari and spread evenly on the baking sheet. Bake for 20 minutes.

Make the cashew-coconut sauce: In a small bowl, whisk together the cashew butter, coconut milk, lime juice, tamari, and sriracha. Set aside.

Kelp noodles require no cooking. Just rinse the noodles under cold water and drain. If using vermicelli rice noodles, prepare the noodles according to the package directions.

In a small skillet, toast the cashews over low heat with a pinch of salt for about 1 minute. Remove from the skillet and set aside.
Wipe out the pan and heat the olive oil over medium-low heat. Add the scallions and sauté until soft and lightly browned, 2 to 3 minutes.

Assemble 4 bowls with a generous slather of sauce on the bottom of each bowl. Evenly distribute the radishes, carrot, cucumber, bean sprouts, noodles, and tofu among the bowls. Add the toasted cashews and scallions to the bowls and top each bowl with cilantro and a sprinkle of red pepper flakes, if using.

Serve with lime wedges, tamari, sriracha, more red pepper flakes, and any remaining sauce on the side.

SERVES 4

VEGAN & GLUTEN-FREE

TIP This recipe will work with spiralized zucchini if you can't find multicolored daikon.

RAINBOW SUMMER VEGGIE SKEWERS

This is the kind of meal I love to make on a Sunday after I've been to the farmers market earlier in the day. Pretty much any summer vegetable that can fit on a skewer is delicious when grilled to charred perfection. This marinade has a nice tang from the rice vinegar but has a deep flavor from the tamari and smoked paprika. Also, don't skip the mushrooms—the sauce soaks into them especially well! Make these skewers a full meal by serving them with the Herbed Farro on page 219.

Marinade

¼ cup tamari

2 tablespoons extra-virgin olive oil

2 tablespoons rice vinegar

2 tablespoons maple syrup

1 teaspoon Dijon mustard

Heaping ½ teaspoon smoked paprika

Freshly ground black pepper

Vegetables

1 yellow squash, cut into 1-inch rounds

1 medium zucchini, cut into 1-inch rounds

8 ounces cremini mushrooms, stemmed

1 small red onion, cut into wedges

1 red bell pepper, cut into 1-inch pieces

1 yellow bell pepper, cut into 1-inch pieces

1 ear fresh corn, cut into 1-inch rounds

1 recipe Healthier Ranch Dressing (page 131), for serving

Herbed Farro (page 219), for serving (optional)

Make the marinade: In a small bowl, whisk together the tamari, olive oil, rice vinegar, maple syrup, mustard, smoked paprika, and a few grinds of black pepper.

Heat a grill to medium-high and spray with nonstick cooking spray. Arrange the vegetables onto metal skewers and brush generously with the marinade so that all sides of each vegetable are well coated. Grill the skewers for 8 minutes per side or until the vegetables are nicely charred.

Drizzle the remaining marinade over the vegetables and serve with the healthier ranch dressing on the side. Serve with the herbed farro, if desired.

Note: *I prefer to use metal skewers because wooden skewers burn easily on the grill.*

SERVES 4   VEGAN   GLUTEN-FREE: Serve with quinoa in place of the farro.

TIP Use any leftover pesto in scrambled eggs the next morning or slathered onto a sandwich for lunch the next day.

SPICY BLACK BEAN & MANGO STUFFED PEPPERS

I've always loved stuffed peppers. Of course, growing up, my sister and I would eat the "stuff" and push aside the pepper. As an adult, I love peppers too much to let them get treated that way, which is why I like to grill my red peppers until they're just tender but not dark and collapsed. After the peppers are lightly charred, I stuff them with this fresh mango and black bean filling and top them with dollops of charred jalapeño pesto for a delicious sweet and spicy combination.

Black Bean & Mango Filling

1½ cups cooked black beans, drained and rinsed (page 23)

1 cup fresh corn kernels

1 ripe mango, peeled, pitted, and diced

1 cup chopped fresh cilantro, including tender stems

Heaping ½ cup crumbled feta cheese

1 tablespoon extra-virgin olive oil

Zest and juice of 1 lime

2 scallions, sliced

1 garlic clove, minced

½ teaspoon chili powder

½ teaspoon sea salt, plus more for sprinkling

Freshly ground black pepper

1 jalapeño, stemmed, seeded, and diced (optional)

For the Peppers

4 red bell peppers, halved, ribbing and seeds removed

Extra-virgin olive oil, for drizzling

Charred Jalapeño Pesto (page 303)

Make the filling: In a large bowl, combine the beans, corn, mango, cilantro, feta, olive oil, lime zest, lime juice, scallions, garlic, chili powder, salt, a few grinds of black pepper, and the jalapeño, if using. Season to taste and set aside.

Heat a grill to medium. Drizzle the red peppers all over with olive oil and sprinkle with salt and pepper. Grill the peppers, cut-side down, for 3 minutes. Turn and grill 3 minutes more. Remove from the grill.

Scoop in the filling and serve with dollops of the jalapeño pesto.

SERVES 4 | VEGAN: Skip the cheese. | GLUTEN-FREE

CREAMY SWEET CORN PAPPARDELLE

There's one food I missed most while living away from Chicago, and it wasn't pizza or hot dogs—it was Midwestern bicolored sweet corn. Now that we're back, I eat as much corn as I can while it's in season. In this pasta, the sweet, juicy corn kernels paired with the "milk" from the cobs become a perfect cream sauce without using actual cream. Cashews add richness, lemon (of course) adds some zing, and paprika adds a smoky depth of flavor.

5 ears corn

2 tablespoons extra-virgin olive oil

½ cup chopped yellow onion

2 garlic cloves, crushed

½ cup raw cashews

¼ cup water, plus more if necessary

2 tablespoons fresh lemon juice

¼ teaspoon smoked paprika

½ teaspoon sea salt, plus more to taste

Freshly ground black pepper

9 ounces pappardelle or pasta of choice

2 scallions, finely sliced

3 packed cups fresh spinach

½ cup sliced fresh basil, for serving (optional)

Microgreens, for serving (optional)

Slice the kernels off the corn cobs, then use the back of a chef's knife to scrape the milky liquid that's left on the cob.

Heat 1 tablespoon of the olive oil in a medium skillet over medium heat. Add the onion and cook until soft, about 3 minutes. Add 1½ cups of the corn and the whole crushed garlic cloves and cook until tender, about 3 minutes more. Transfer to a blender and add the milky corn liquid, cashews, water, lemon juice, smoked paprika, salt, and a few grinds of black pepper. Blend until creamy, adding more water as needed to create a pourable consistency. Set aside.

Bring a large pot of salted water to a boil. Prepare the pasta according to the instructions on the package, cooking until al dente. Reserve ¾ cup of the hot pasta water, then drain.

Meanwhile, wipe out the skillet and heat the remaining 1 tablespoon olive oil over medium heat. Add the remaining corn, the scallions, a pinch of salt, and a few grinds of black pepper and cook, stirring occasionally, until tender, about 3 minutes. Add the spinach, cooked pasta, the corn sauce, and ½ to ¾ cup of the reserved pasta water, as needed to create a creamy sauce. Season to taste and serve immediately with the sliced basil and microgreens, if using.

SERVES 4   VEGAN: Use eggless pasta.   GLUTEN-FREE: Use gluten-free pasta.

VEGETARIAN PORTOBELLO REUBEN SANDWICHES

The reuben is Jack's favorite sandwich of all time. I set out to create this recipe with him in mind, but it ended up as one of my favorite recipes in this book as well. A portobello mushroom replaces the meat, but this is no ordinary mushroom sandwich. The creamy horseradish sauce is tangy and delectable, and the pickled cabbage provides a bright pop of flavor next to the deeply savory balsamic mushrooms. The components take a little time to prepare, but you can make them days in advance for faster sandwich assembly.

———◆◆———

Pickled Red Cabbage*

1½ cups packed shredded red cabbage

½ cup thinly sliced red onion

1 garlic clove, smashed

1 teaspoon sea salt

¾ cup apple cider vinegar

¾ cup water

½ teaspoon caraway seeds

1 teaspoon cane sugar

If you make the pickled cabbage in advance, it'll keep in the fridge for at least 2 weeks.

Horseradish Sauce (makes extra)

½ cup raw cashews

¼ cup plus 2 tablespoons water

2 tablespoons fresh lemon juice

2 tablespoons Dijon mustard

1½ tablespoons ketchup

1 tablespoon dill pickle relish

1½ teaspoons jarred horseradish

1 small garlic clove

¼ teaspoon sea salt

Sandwiches

4 portobello mushrooms, stemmed

Extra-virgin olive oil, for drizzling

Balsamic vinegar, for drizzling

Sea salt and freshly ground black pepper

8 slices rye bread

4 slices Swiss cheese

1½ cups arugula

recipe continues

Make the pickled red cabbage: Place the cabbage, onion, garlic, and salt in a 16-ounce lidded jar. In a small pot over medium heat, simmer the apple cider vinegar, water, caraway seeds, and sugar until the sugar is dissolved, about 1 minute. Pour the brine over the cabbage mixture in the jar. Cover, shake gently, then uncover and let cool to room temperature. Chill for at least 1 hour.

Make the horseradish sauce: In a blender, place the cashews, water, lemon juice, mustard, ketchup, relish, horseradish, garlic, and salt. Blend until smooth.

Preheat a grill pan. Drizzle both sides of the mushrooms with olive oil and balsamic vinegar, using your hands to make sure they are well coated. Season generously with salt and pepper. Grill the mushrooms, 5 to 7 minutes per side, until browned and soft. Remove from the heat, transfer to a cutting board, and slice into ¼-inch strips.

Preheat the oven to 400°F and line a large baking sheet with parchment paper. Place the bread slices on the baking sheet. Layer 4 of them with the sauce, the sliced grilled mushrooms, and the cheese. Bake all the bread slices for 4 to 6 minutes or until the cheese is melted and the 4 bare bread slices are lightly toasted.

Remove the baking sheet from the oven and top the sandwiches with a scoop of the drained pickled cabbage and the arugula. Spread the sauce on the remaining toasted bread, top each sandwich, slice in half, and serve.

SERVES 4		VEGAN: Skip the cheese and serve with extra sauce.	GLUTEN-FREE: Use gluten-free bread.

TIP This recipe makes extra sauce, and the sauce keeps well in the fridge for up to a week. I love this sandwich so much that I'll grill up more mushrooms a few days later and enjoy it all over again!

CHICKPEA HARISSA VEGGIE BURGERS

Years ago, when I first became vegetarian, I'd always buy prepackaged veggie burgers that tasted like cardboard and smother them with enough toppings to hide the taste. This recipe offers something completely different and completely satisfying—unlike those burgers, these have a wonderful hearty texture, and their spicy, smoky flavor from harissa, cumin, and paprika makes them bolder and more exciting than any veggie burger I've had before. Skip the ketchup and mustard here—the Creamy Cilantro Sauce takes seconds to make, and it accents the burgers perfectly!

Burgers

1 tablespoon ground flaxseed

3 tablespoons water

1 tablespoon extra-virgin olive oil, plus more for drizzling

½ yellow onion, diced (1 cup)

½ teaspoon sea salt, plus more to taste

1 cup chopped walnuts

2 teaspoons ground cumin

2 teaspoons smoked paprika

½ teaspoon freshly ground black pepper

3 garlic cloves, minced

¼ cup Homemade Harissa (page 281), or store-bought

1½ cups cooked chickpeas, drained and rinsed (page 23), divided

1 cup cooked short-grain brown rice (page 22)*

2 tablespoons fresh lime juice

⅓ cup panko bread crumbs

It's very important that your brown rice is freshly made and sticky so that the burgers will be cohesive. Because long-grain rice isn't as sticky, be sure to use short-grain rice.

Creamy Cilantro Sauce

½ cup mayonnaise

½ garlic clove, minced

¼ cup chopped fresh cilantro leaves and stems

½ teaspoon lime zest

1 teaspoon fresh lime juice

Sea salt and freshly ground black pepper

For Serving

6 whole-grain hamburger buns, toasted

Thinly sliced red onion

Arugula

Cucumber Dill or Yellow Squash Pickles (page 297, optional)

recipe continues

In a small bowl, whisk together the ground flaxseed and water. Set aside.

Make the creamy cilantro sauce: In a small bowl, stir together the mayo, garlic, cilantro, and lime zest and juice and season with salt and pepper. Chill until ready to use.

Make the burgers: Heat the olive oil in a medium pan over medium heat. Add the onion and salt and cook until soft, about 5 minutes. Add the walnuts, cumin, paprika, pepper, and garlic. Stir to combine and remove the pan from the heat. Let the mixture cool slightly, then place the mixture in a food processor along with the harissa and half of the chickpeas. Pulse until everything is well combined but still chunky. Do not puree.

Transfer the mixture to a large bowl and add the remaining chickpeas, the brown rice, and the lime juice. Use a potato masher and mash until everything is well combined. Stir in the panko and the flaxseed mixture. Form the mixture into 6 patties.

Heat a grill to high or preheat the oven to 425°F. Drizzle the burgers with olive oil. Spray the grill grates with nonstick cooking spray or line a baking sheet with parchment paper. Grill the burgers for 5 minutes per side, or until dark char marks form, turning gently. If using the oven, bake the burgers on the baking sheet for 9 minutes per side.

Serve the burgers on the hamburger buns. Slather with the creamy cilantro sauce and assemble with red onion, arugula, and pickles, as desired.

SERVES 6 | **VEGAN:** Use vegan mayo. | **GLUTEN-FREE:** Use gluten-free panko.

ZUCCHINI NOODLE PUTTANESCA

This recipe did the impossible—it got Jack and me to love olives! I've always had a difficult time cooking with olives, as their flavor tends to dominate any dish. In this recipe, the olives work harmoniously with the other briny elements, and the zucchini noodles make me feel light and bright on a warm summer night.

3 medium zucchini

1 tablespoon extra-virgin olive oil

1 shallot, minced (⅓ cup)

1 medium Italian eggplant, chopped into ½-inch cubes (4 cups)

2 cups halved cherry tomatoes

Sea salt and freshly ground black pepper

¼ cup dry white wine

2 garlic cloves, minced

⅓ cup chopped oil-packed sun-dried tomatoes

½ teaspoon red pepper flakes

½ tablespoon capers

2 teaspoons lemon zest

⅓ cup chopped kalamata olives

½ cup sliced fresh basil

2 tablespoons pine nuts

Easy Quinoa Sage Veggie Balls (page 277), for serving

Spiralize the zucchini and set aside.

In a large nonstick skillet, heat the olive oil over medium heat. Add the shallot, eggplant, tomatoes, a generous pinch of salt, and a few grinds of black pepper. Cook until soft, shaking the pan occasionally, 5 to 8 minutes. Reduce the heat if necessary.

Stir in the wine, garlic, sun-dried tomatoes, red pepper flakes, and capers and cook until the liquid is reduced by half, 2 to 3 minutes. Stir in the lemon zest and olives.

Add the zucchini noodles to the pan. Toss until the zucchini is just warmed through, about 1 minute (it will turn soft and watery if cooked longer). Season to taste. Serve with the basil, pine nuts, and the quinoa sage veggie balls.

SERVES 4 | VEGAN | GLUTEN-FREE: Use gluten-free panko in the veggie balls.

TIP Don't skip the quinoa sage veggie balls. Their hearty, savory quality works perfectly in this bright dish.

MEDITERRANEAN STUFFED EGGPLANT

This recipe can be made two ways—grilled or baked. I can't decide which version I like better, so the choice is up to you! Since eggplants are in season from late summer to early fall, I grill at the beginning of the season when the nights are hot and bake near the end on cool fall evenings.

3 medium eggplants
(12 to 15 ounces each)

2 tablespoons extra-virgin olive oil, plus more for drizzling

¼ to ½ teaspoon sea salt, plus more for sprinkling

Freshly ground black pepper

2 cups cooked bulgur (page 22)

2 garlic cloves, minced

1 tablespoon sherry vinegar

⅓ cup chopped oil-packed sun-dried tomatoes

1 cup cooked French green lentils (page 23)*

½ cup chopped pine nuts

½ cup chopped fresh parsley

¼ teaspoon red pepper flakes

For the Grilled Version

1½ cups chopped arugula

¾ cup chopped basil

For the Baked Version

¼ cup panko bread crumbs

¼ cup shredded pecorino cheese (optional)

Be sure to seek out French green lentils for this recipe. They hold their shape when cooked until al dente. Regular green or brown lentils tend to become mushy when cooked.

Heat a grill to medium. If baking, preheat the oven to 400°F and line a baking sheet with parchment paper.

Slice the eggplants in half lengthwise and scoop out the flesh, leaving a ½-inch rim around the edges. Drizzle the eggplant shells with olive oil and season with pinches of salt and a few grinds of black pepper. Grill, cut-side down, for 15 minutes or until tender and softened but still holding their shape. Alternatively, bake cut-side down on the baking sheet for 20 to 30 minutes.

In a large bowl, toss the cooked bulgur with the garlic, 2 tablespoons olive oil, the sherry vinegar, sun-dried tomatoes, lentils, pine nuts, parsley, ¼ teaspoon sea salt, and red pepper flakes.

IF GRILLING:

Add the chopped arugula and basil to the stuffing mixture and fill the eggplants. Season with additional salt, if desired.

IF BAKING:

Fill the eggplant with the stuffing mixture and top with the panko and pecorino cheese, if using. Broil for 4 to 8 minutes or until golden brown on top.

SERVES 6

VEGAN: Skip the cheese.

GLUTEN-FREE: Use quinoa in place of the bulgur and use gluten-free panko.

LEEK & RADISH GREEN TART

The more I fall in love with vegetables, the more I love figuring out clever ways to use the tops, greens, and scraps that are commonly tossed out. Who decided we should throw these things away anyway? This recipe uses the whole radish— the greens are baked into the tart filling, and the radishes are diced into a lively lemony salad. This recipe is wonderful for a spring brunch or dinner.

———◆◆———

8 large eggs

¼ cup unsweetened almond milk

2 tablespoons minced tarragon

½ teaspoon Dijon mustard

½ teaspoon sea salt, plus more to taste

Freshly ground black pepper

½ teaspoon extra-virgin olive oil

1 leek, white and light green parts only, halved, thinly sliced, and rinsed well

2 packed cups radish greens

1 garlic clove, minced

1 recipe Vegan Pie Crust (page 289)

Radish Salad

8 red radishes, sliced into matchsticks

1 cup peas, blanched 1 minute if fresh, thawed if frozen

¼ cup chopped fresh mint leaves

3 tablespoons crumbled feta cheese

1 tablespoon fresh lemon juice

1 tablespoon minced chives

Sea salt and freshly ground black pepper

In a large bowl, whisk together the eggs, almond milk, tarragon, mustard, salt, and several grinds of black pepper. Set aside.

Heat the olive oil in a medium skillet over medium heat. Add the leeks and a pinch of salt and sauté until soft, 1 minute. Add the radish greens and garlic and sauté until the greens are wilted, about 1 minute. Transfer to a plate and set aside.

When the tart crust is finished prebaking, fold the radish greens/leek mixture into the egg mixture and pour into the crust. Bake for 18 to 20 minutes or until the eggs are set.

Make the radish salad: In a medium bowl, combine the sliced radishes, peas, mint, feta cheese, lemon juice, chives, and salt and pepper to taste.

Serve tart slices with scoops of radish salad on top.

If using a standard pie pan, form the sides of the crust three-quarters of the way up the sides of the pan. Increase baking time to 25 to 28 minutes.

SERVES 6 TO 8

TIP
The pie dough can be made up to 1 day in advance and stored in the refrigerator. When ready to use, let it sit at room temperature until pliable, 30 to 45 minutes.

PIZZA WITH APPLES, LEEKS & LEMON ZEST LABNEH

If you're a plain-cheese-pizza kind of person, you may want to turn the page. This pizza is full of so many unique flavors and textures, and we're pretty obsessed with it. A layer of cheese holds together the sautéed leeks, apples, and fresh thyme. The best part is the tangy homemade lemon zest labneh, which (heads up!) needs to be made the day before. If you forget, use a mild goat cheese in its place.

---

2 cups diced leeks, white and light green parts (1 to 2 leeks)

2 teaspoons extra-virgin olive oil, plus more for drizzling and brushing

1 Gala apple, finely diced

1 recipe Homemade Pizza Dough (page 291), or fresh store-bought

1½ cups white cheddar cheese

2 tablespoons fresh thyme leaves

Lemon Zest Labneh (page 295; make 1 day ahead)

¼ cup microgreens or ½ cup arugula

Sea salt and freshly ground black pepper

Rinse the diced leeks and set on a kitchen towel to dry.

In a large skillet, heat the olive oil over medium heat. Add the leeks and a few pinches of salt and sauté for 2 minutes. Add the apple, reduce the heat to medium-low, and stir until softened, about 3 minutes more. Remove from the heat and set aside.

Preheat the oven to 500°F. Roll out the pizza dough to fit a 14-inch round pizza pan and prebake the dough for 5 minutes. Remove from the oven and top with the cheese and the sautéed leeks and apples. Drizzle lightly with olive oil and brush the edges of the crust with a bit of oil. Bake for 12 minutes or until the toppings and edges of the crust are golden brown.

Remove from the oven and top with the fresh thyme, dollops of the labneh, a drizzle of olive oil, and the microgreens. Season to taste and serve.

SERVES 2 OR 3

183

TIP Make sure your pan is not too hot when you add the yogurt sauce so that the yogurt doesn't separate.

GREEK YOGURT SAAG PANEER

Whenever we go out for Indian food, Jack orders saag paneer. He's crazy for creamed spinach, and I'm crazy for making a completely inauthentic version of a popular dish, but we love this fresh take. I use fresh whole-leaf spinach and cook it until it's barely wilted before mixing it with a lemony cardamom-spiced Greek yogurt sauce. I usually find paneer at Whole Foods, but halloumi also works in a pinch, as does seared extra-firm tofu.

Heaping ½ cup whole milk Greek yogurt

1 teaspoon fresh lemon juice, plus 4 lemon wedges for serving

½ teaspoon ground cardamom

½ teaspoon sea salt, plus more to taste

Freshly ground black pepper

2 tablespoons coconut oil

8 ounces paneer cheese, cubed

1 medium yellow onion, chopped

½ cup water, as needed

1 tablespoon whole cumin seeds

2 garlic cloves, minced

1 teaspoon minced fresh ginger

1 teaspoon mild curry powder

16 ounces fresh spinach

3 cups cooked brown rice (page 22)

½ cup chopped fresh cilantro

Sliced serrano pepper (optional)

Red pepper flakes (optional)

½ cup fresh microgreens (optional)

In a small bowl, mix together the yogurt, lemon juice, cardamom, ¼ teaspoon of the salt, and a few grinds of black pepper. Set aside.

Heat a cast-iron skillet over medium heat, then add 1 tablespoon of the coconut oil and the paneer. Cook for 1 minute per side or until browned, reducing the heat if necessary. Transfer to a plate and sprinkle with a few pinches of salt.

In a large, deep skillet, heat the remaining 1 tablespoon coconut oil over medium-low heat. Add the onion and the remaining ¼ teaspoon salt and cook for 12 minutes, or until the onion is well browned. Set the water nearby. If the pan becomes dry during the next few steps, add water, a few tablespoons at a time. Stir in the cumin seeds and cook for 1 minute. Reduce the heat and stir in the garlic, ginger, and curry powder. Add the spinach, stir, and cook until wilted, about 2 minutes, working in batches if necessary. Remove the pan from the heat, let cool slightly, and stir in the yogurt mixture until just warmed through (you don't want to cook it too much or the yogurt will separate).

Divide the rice among four bowls. Top each bowl with the spinach mixture, the paneer, and a squeeze of lemon juice. Serve with the cilantro, serrano pepper, red pepper flakes, and microgreens, if desired, and extra lemon wedges on the side.

SERVES 4

GLUTEN-FREE

TURMERIC-SPICED WHOLE ROASTED CAULIFLOWER

My family loved this recipe while I was creating it. Having grown up in a traditional meat-and-potatoes household, I could have never imagined the day that my mother, father, myself, and Jack would all gather around the dinner table to a giant cauliflower "Sunday roast."

1 medium cauliflower (2 pounds)

3 tablespoons extra-virgin olive oil, plus more for drizzling

Sea salt and freshly ground black pepper

2 tablespoons fresh lemon juice, plus more to taste

4 cups mixed spring greens

½ cup chopped mixed fresh herbs (cilantro, mint, parsley)

¼ cup toasted pine nuts or slivered almonds

Spiced Turmeric Sauce

½ cup whole milk Greek yogurt

2 tablespoons extra-virgin olive oil

2 tablespoons fresh lemon juice

1 garlic clove, minced

¼ teaspoon ground cumin

¼ teaspoon ground coriander

¼ teaspoon ground turmeric

¼ teaspoon maple syrup or honey

½ teaspoon sea salt

Pinch of cayenne pepper

Preheat the oven to 400°F and loosely line a baking sheet with aluminum foil.

Slice the bottom of the core off the cauliflower so that it sits evenly on the baking sheet. Drizzle 1½ tablespoons of the olive oil over the cauliflower and use your hands to coat it evenly. Sprinkle with salt and pepper and roast for 45 minutes.

Make the sauce: In a small bowl, combine the yogurt, olive oil, lemon juice, garlic, cumin, coriander, turmeric, maple syrup, salt, and cayenne.

Remove the cauliflower from the oven and use a fork to gently start to pull apart its crevices. Pour another 1½ tablespoons of olive oil and the lemon juice over the cauliflower, especially into the crevices, and roast for another 15 minutes.

Remove the cauliflower from the oven and spread one-quarter of the yogurt sauce all over. Roast for another 15 minutes.

In a large bowl, toss the spring greens with a drizzle of olive oil, a squeeze of lemon, and a pinch of salt.

Remove the cauliflower from the oven. It should be tender outside and fork-tender inside. Top the cauliflower with more sauce and sprinkle with the herbs and toasted pine nuts. Slice into quarters and serve with the salad and the remaining sauce on the side.

SERVES 4

GLUTEN-FREE

RUTABAGA WALNUT RAGU

I've made vegetarian ragu-type sauces in the past by using mushrooms and lentils.
I love *this* one because it uses the most ugly and underutilized vegetable—the rutabaga.
Don't let the rutabaga's pungent smell scare you, because the bitterness will cook off once
combined with the sweet onions, carrots, flavorful sun-dried tomatoes, red wine, and a good
amount of fresh sage and rosemary. The walnuts add a nice meaty texture to this hearty dish.

◆

1 tablespoon extra-virgin olive oil,
plus more for drizzling

½ medium yellow onion, finely diced

2 small carrots, finely diced

1 celery stalk, finely diced

1 medium rutabaga, peeled and finely
diced (¾ cup)

Sea salt and freshly ground black pepper

¼ cup diced oil-packed sun-dried
tomatoes

3 tablespoons minced fresh sage

1 teaspoon minced fresh rosemary

3 garlic cloves, minced

½ cup crushed walnuts

¼ cup dry red wine

1 tablespoon balsamic vinegar

½ teaspoon red pepper flakes, plus more
to taste

Pinch of saffron in 1 teaspoon warm water

8 ounces rigatoni pasta

⅓ cup fresh leafy herbs (parsley, basil,
or oregano), diced if large

Grated Parmesan cheese, for serving
(optional)

Heat the olive oil in a large skillet over
medium heat. Add the onion, carrots, celery,
rutabaga, a few generous pinches of salt,
and a few grinds of black pepper and cook,
stirring occasionally, until soft and browned,
about 15 minutes.

Reduce the heat to low and stir in the sun-
dried tomatoes, sage, rosemary, garlic, and
walnuts until incorporated. Stir in the wine
and balsamic vinegar and let it simmer and
bubble for about 30 seconds, until reduced
by half. Turn off the heat and stir in the red
pepper flakes and saffron.

Meanwhile, bring a large pot of salted water
to a boil. Prepare the pasta according to the
package directions, cooking until al dente.
Reserve ½ cup of the hot pasta water, then
drain. Add the pasta to the pan with the
vegetables, along with ¼ to ½ cup of the
reserved pasta water, enough to create a
loose sauce. Toss together until the pasta is
well coated. Season to taste with more salt
and pepper.

Serve with a drizzle of olive oil, the fresh
herbs, and Parmesan cheese, if desired.

SERVES 4 | **VEGAN:** Skip the cheese. | **GLUTEN-FREE:** Use gluten-free pasta.

QUINOA, APPLE & SAGE STUFFED ACORN SQUASH

This is everything I crave on the first day of fall. Once the temps start to drop, I love cooking dinner to the warm and cozy scent of squash roasting away in the oven. The squash becomes a veritable cornucopia, filled with fall ingredients tossed with a sweet and savory apple cider sage vinaigrette.

※

2 acorn squash

Extra-virgin olive oil, for drizzling

½ teaspoon sea salt, plus more to taste

Freshly ground black pepper

2 cups cooked quinoa (page 22)

5 lacinato kale leaves, stems removed, very finely chopped (2 cups)

3 scallions, sliced

1 Gala apple, finely diced

⅓ cup chopped toasted hazelnuts

⅓ cup pomegranate seeds

⅓ cup crumbled feta cheese (optional)

Dressing

¼ cup extra-virgin olive oil

2 tablespoons apple cider vinegar

2 teaspoons maple syrup

½ teaspoon cinnamon

16 sage leaves, chopped (about ¼ cup)

½ teaspoon sea salt

Freshly ground black pepper

Preheat the oven to 425°F and line a baking sheet with parchment paper.

Slice the acorn squash in half and scoop out the seeds. Slice the halves into quarters and drizzle with olive oil, a pinch of salt, and a few grinds of black pepper. Place the squash pieces cut-side down and roast for 40 to 55 minutes or until tender and golden.

Make the dressing: In a small saucepan over low heat, gently heat the olive oil, apple cider vinegar, and maple syrup until warm. Add the cinnamon, sage, salt, and a few grinds of black pepper and stir until fragrant, about 30 seconds.

In a large bowl, mix together the quinoa, kale, scallions, and diced apple and toss with half the dressing. Add the hazelnuts, pomegranate seeds, salt, and a few grinds of black pepper and toss again.

Assemble the squash on a platter. Scoop the filling into the squash, top with the feta, if using, drizzle with the remaining dressing, and serve.

SERVES 6 TO 8

VEGAN & GLUTEN-FREE

SUNSHINE
SWEET POTATO CURRY

This curry's yellow color and bold flavor put me in a happy, sunny mood
when it's gloomy and cold outside. The secret to that color and flavor?
Sweet potato is blended into the sauce itself, coating the curry vegetables
in a naturally sweet and rich golden sauce that will brighten up any day.

Sweet Potato Yellow Curry Sauce

1 small sweet potato

1 teaspoon whole cumin seeds

1 teaspoon coriander seeds

10 cardamom pods, seeds removed

1½ cups full-fat canned coconut milk

2 garlic cloves

1 tablespoon grated fresh ginger

½ teaspoon ground turmeric

¼ teaspoon cayenne pepper

Zest of 1 lime

½ teaspoon white wine vinegar

½ teaspoon sea salt

Curry Vegetables

1 tablespoon coconut oil

½ medium yellow onion, chopped

½ teaspoon sea salt, plus more to taste

Freshly ground black pepper

1 red pepper, stem and seeds removed,
julienned

1 small sweet potato, chopped into 1-inch
cubes

½ medium cauliflower (about 3 cups
florets)

½ jalapeño pepper, diced, or 1 serrano,
thinly sliced

1 cup cooked chickpeas, drained and
rinsed (page 23)

6 cups packed baby spinach

Juice of 1 lime, plus extra wedges
for serving

For Serving

3 cups cooked basmati rice (page 22)

½ cup chopped fresh cilantro

¼ cup crushed toasted cashews

recipe continues

Make the sweet potato yellow curry sauce: Preheat the oven to 425°F. Use a fork to poke a few holes in the sweet potato and roast for 60 minutes, or until soft. Measure ½ cup of the cooked soft flesh.

Toast the cumin, coriander, and cardamom in a small dry skillet over medium heat, until they begin to pop, 2 to 3 minutes.

In a blender, place the ½ cup sweet potato flesh, the toasted spices, coconut milk, garlic, ginger, turmeric, cayenne, lime zest, vinegar, and salt. Blend until smooth.

Prepare the curry vegetables: Heat the oil in a large Dutch oven over medium-low heat.

Add the onion, salt, and a few grinds of black pepper and sauté until soft, about 8 minutes. Add the red pepper, sweet potato, cauliflower, jalapeño, and three-quarters of the sauce. Stir to combine. Reduce the heat to low and simmer, covered, stirring occasionally, for 18 to 22 minutes, or until the sweet potatoes are tender.

Stir in the chickpeas and spinach. Cover and let cook for 5 minutes more, until the spinach is wilted. Stir in the lime juice and season to taste with more salt and black pepper.

Serve the curry with the basmati rice, the remaining sauce, cilantro, toasted cashews, and lime wedges.

SERVES 4   VEGAN & GLUTEN-FREE

TIP   This curry is wonderful left over—in fact, it's probably better on the second day. It also freezes well.

KALE & SWEET POTATO LASAGNA ROLL-UPS

Everyone loves lasagna on a cold night, and this rolled-up version makes the classic dish even more fun! I love my lasagna full of veggies, of course. Here, sweet potato and kale play off the creamy vegan ricotta and fresh sage to create delightful bites full of contrasting textures and cozy, savory flavor. As an added bonus, this lasagna is easy to serve—no slicing necessary!

1 large sweet potato, cut into small cubes

Extra-virgin olive oil, for drizzling

Sea salt and freshly ground black pepper

6 kale leaves, torn, coarse stems removed

12 lasagna noodles, plus 2 extra in case of breakage

2½ cups Marinara Sauce (page 298)

2 recipes (3 cups) Vegan Ricotta (page 285)

¼ cup minced sage

Pinches of red pepper flakes

Preheat the oven to 425°F and line a large baking sheet with parchment paper. Place the sweet potato cubes on the baking sheet and toss with a drizzle of olive oil and pinches of salt and pepper. Roast 25 to 30 minutes, or until golden brown.

Fill a large pot with 1 inch of water and insert a steamer basket. Add the kale and bring to a boil. Cover and steam for 1 minute, or until just wilted. Scoop the kale onto a kitchen towel and squeeze out the excess water.

Bring a large pot of heavily salted water to a boil. Prepare the pasta according to the instructions on the package, cooking until al dente. Be careful not to overcook or the curly edges may fall apart. Drain.

Brush the bottom of a 9x13-inch baking dish with a little olive oil and spread with 1 cup of the marinara.

Lay the first 6 noodles side-by-side onto a large baking sheet. Gently toss the remainder of the noodles with a little olive oil so they don't stick together. Spread 3 to 4 tablespoons of the ricotta onto each noodle, dot the kale and sweet potatoes evenly on top and sprinkle with the sage and red pepper flakes. Roll each noodle. Place each lasagna roll into the baking dish, seam-side down. Repeat with the remaining 6 noodles.

Spoon the remaining marinara on top of the rolls. Cover and bake for 20 minutes.

SERVES 4

VEGAN

MOJO BLACK BEAN BOWLS WITH SWISS CHARD

The red pepper sauce used here is one to keep on hand at all times. It's bold, it's punchy, and it's wonderful drizzled on just about any vegetable. I can think of so many combinations of bowls that would be delicious doused with this sauce, but I love this bean, greens, rice, and crispy potato bowl. The toasted spicy pepitas are not only a tasty topping but a highly addictive snack. Try not to eat them all as they come out of the oven!

———◆———

1 pound small potatoes, quartered

1 tablespoon extra-virgin olive oil, plus more for drizzling

½ teaspoon sea salt, plus more for sprinkling

Freshly ground black pepper

2 scallions, sliced

1 garlic clove, minced

½ to 1 jalapeño pepper, stemmed, seeded, and diced

1 bunch Swiss chard, leaves chopped, stems finely chopped

1 cup cilantro stems, finely diced

2 tablespoons fresh lime juice

1½ cups cooked black beans, drained and rinsed (page 23)

2 cups cooked brown rice (page 22)

1 recipe Red Pepper Mojo Sauce (page 131)

½ cup crumbled feta cheese (optional)

Spicy Pepitas

½ cup pepitas

½ teaspoon tamari

Pinch of chili powder

Pinch of cayenne pepper

Preheat the oven to 425°F and line 2 baking sheets with parchment paper.

Place the potatoes on one baking sheet and toss with a generous drizzle of olive oil, generous pinches of salt, and a few grinds of black pepper. Roast for 35 minutes, or until the potatoes are browned and crispy around the edges. When the potatoes are done roasting, reduce the heat to 350°F. Set the potatoes aside.

Make the spicy pepitas: On the second baking sheet, combine the pepitas with the tamari, chili powder, and cayenne. Toss to coat, then spread out onto the sheet. Bake for 5 minutes, or until browned and crispy. Set aside.

Heat the olive oil in a large skillet over medium heat. Add the scallions, garlic, jalapeño, chard stems, and cilantro stems and sauté until softened, 3 to 4 minutes. Stir in the chard leaves and cook until just wilted, 1 to 2 minutes. Remove from the heat and stir in the lime juice, black beans, salt, and a few grinds of black pepper.

Assemble the bowls with the rice, chard mixture, roasted potatoes, and generous drizzles of the red pepper mojo sauce. Top with the feta cheese, if using, and the spicy pepitas.

SERVES 4   VEGAN: Skip the cheese.   GLUTEN-FREE

TIP   Bake extra spicy pepitas for snacking.

LEMON RISOTTO WITH TRUMPET MUSHROOM "SCALLOPS"

Jack has only a few signature dishes, but once he claims a certain recipe or method, he works on it to perfection and it's "his" to make forever. For a long time, our date-night-in meal was risotto and scallops. I'd make the risotto, and he'd perfectly sear scallops. I thought it'd be fun to make veggie "scallops" out of trumpet mushrooms and serve them over risotto, just like we used to make. This recipe is a great one to make with your partner—one person can be the risotto stirrer while the other tends to the mushrooms.

Trumpet Mushroom Scallops

1 tablespoon extra-virgin olive oil

5 trumpet mushrooms, sliced into ½-inch rounds

¼ teaspoon sea salt

1 teaspoon balsamic vinegar

Freshly ground black pepper

Risotto

1 tablespoon extra-virgin olive oil

2 cups chopped leeks, white and light green parts only, rinsed well

¼ teaspoon sea salt, plus more to taste

Freshly ground black pepper

2 garlic cloves, minced

½ cup uncooked Arborio rice, rinsed

½ cup dry white wine

4 cups Vegetable Broth (page 104), at room temperature

½ cup fresh or frozen peas

¼ cup freshly grated Parmesan or pecorino cheese, plus more for serving (optional)

2 teaspoons lemon zest, half reserved for garnish

1 tablespoon fresh lemon juice

¼ cup chopped fresh mixed herbs (parsley, basil, and/or tarragon), some reserved for garnish

2 tablespoons chopped chives, half reserved for garnish

recipe continues

Make the trumpet mushroom scallops: Heat the olive oil in a large cast-iron skillet. Add the mushrooms, salt, and several grinds of black pepper and toss to coat. Cook for 15 minutes, tossing only occasionally, so that the mushrooms sear against the heat of the pan. Remove the pan from the heat, stir in the balsamic vinegar, and set aside.

Make the risotto: Heat the olive oil in a large skillet over medium heat. Add the leeks and season with the salt and a few grinds of pepper. Cook for 4 to 5 minutes or until soft. Add the garlic and stir to incorporate. Stir in the rice and let it cook for 1 minute. Stir in the wine and cook for another 1 to 2 minutes, or until the wine cooks down.

Add the broth, ¾ cup at a time, stirring continuously between each addition. Allow each addition of broth to be absorbed by the rice before adding the next. Cook until the rice is al dente. The risotto should be soft and creamy. Stir in the peas and cook until warmed through. Stir in the cheese, if using, 1 teaspoon of the lemon zest, the lemon juice, mixed herbs, and chives.

Season to taste and serve with the mushrooms on top. Garnish with the reserved lemon zest, mixed herbs, and chives. Serve with additional grated cheese, if desired.

SERVES 4

VEGAN: Skip the cheese. **GLUTEN-FREE**

TIP If your grits become too thick, whisk in more water and/or a few drizzles of olive oil to reach your desired consistency.

SAUCY MUSHROOMS & CREAMY GRITS BOWLS

In the breakfast chapter, I shared my trick for quick-cooking polenta (page 49), and I use the same technique with grits here. Giving the coarse grains a few pulses in the blender and soaking them overnight may sound fussy, but at dinnertime, your grits will be cooked to creamy perfection in about 7 minutes. If you can't find grits, use polenta—they're interchangeable.

Creamy Grits

1 cup grits

3 cups water

2 tablespoons extra-virgin olive oil

¼ cup pecorino cheese

½ teaspoon sea salt, plus more to taste

Freshly ground black pepper

Mushrooms

2 tablespoons extra-virgin olive oil

24 ounces mixed mushrooms, stemmed and quartered

2 shallots, chopped

1 teaspoon sea salt

Freshly ground black pepper

1 cup white wine

2 garlic cloves, minced

2 tablespoons tomato paste

2 cups Vegetable Broth (page 104)

1 bundle fresh thyme (16 sprigs)

For Serving

Extra-virgin olive oil, for brushing

4 large eggs

1 tablespoon finely minced tarragon

1 tablespoon finely minced parsley

Microgreens, for garnish (optional)

Prepare the grits: In a blender, process the dry grits until the granules are very fine. Transfer to a large jar, stir in 1 cup of the water, and refrigerate overnight. This helps the grits soften and makes them quick to cook.

Prepare the mushrooms: Heat the olive oil in a large, deep skillet over medium heat. Add the mushrooms, shallots, salt, and a few grinds of pepper, and stir until browned and softened, 6 to 8 minutes. Stir in the wine, garlic, and tomato paste. Let the wine reduce by half, 30 seconds to 1 minute. Add the broth and thyme sprigs, then reduce the heat to low and simmer, stirring occasionally, for 6 to 8 minutes, until thickened. Turn off the heat and set aside.

Make the grits: Pour the grits and their soaking water into a medium saucepan. Add the remaining 2 cups water and bring to a gentle boil. Reduce the heat to a simmer and cook, whisking occasionally, for 5 to 7 minutes, until thickened. Stir in the olive oil, cheese, salt, and black pepper to taste.

Brush a large nonstick skillet with olive oil and heat over low heat. Crack or pour in the eggs, cover, and continue to cook over low heat until the yolks are set.

Assemble bowls with the grits, mushrooms, and eggs. Top with the minced tarragon, parsley, and microgreens, if using. Season to taste and serve.

SERVES 4

VEGAN: Skip the cheese, skip the egg, and season the grits with a bit more salt.

GLUTEN-FREE

ROOT VEGETABLE TAGINE WITH LEMON COUSCOUS

When we visited Marrakech, it was July and 114°F. However, that didn't stop the locals from serving us warm, stewy tagine. Eating hot comfort food when it's hot outside sounds weird, and it was. It was also delicious. My version is anything but traditional, but this warmly spiced root vegetable stew is what I now crave when winter rolls around and I'm ready to curl up on the couch. Made with dried apricots, it has a light sweetness that's balanced by the bright lemon couscous. Serve this dish with a scoop of harissa (page 281) for an extra pop of flavor.

1 teaspoon ground cumin

1 teaspoon ground coriander

½ teaspoon cinnamon

½ teaspoon red pepper flakes

1 tablespoon extra-virgin olive oil

1 small yellow onion, chopped into 1-inch pieces

½ teaspoon sea salt, plus more to taste

2 garlic cloves, minced

1 teaspoon grated fresh ginger

1½ cups Vegetable Broth (page 104)

8 dried apricots, diced

2 medium sweet potatoes, cut into large 1-inch pieces

2 large parsnips or carrots, cut into large 1-inch pieces

1½ cups cooked chickpeas, drained and rinsed (page 23)

2 tablespoons fresh lemon juice, plus lemon wedges for serving

Freshly ground black pepper

½ cup chopped fresh parsley

¼ cup sliced almonds, toasted

Homemade Harissa (page 281), for serving (optional)

Lemon Couscous

1 cup uncooked Israeli couscous

½ teaspoon extra-virgin olive oil

1 tablespoon fresh lemon juice

½ teaspoon lemon zest (or ½ tablespoon chopped Quick Preserved Lemons, page 279)

½ cup chopped fresh parsley and/or fresh cilantro

Sea salt and freshly ground black pepper

recipe continues

In a small bowl, mix together the cumin, coriander, cinnamon, and red pepper flakes and set aside.

Heat the olive oil in a medium pot or Dutch oven over medium heat. Add the onion and the salt and cook until soft, about 5 minutes.

Reduce the heat to low and stir in the garlic, ginger, and dried spices. Add the broth, apricots, sweet potatoes, parsnips, and chickpeas. Bring to a gentle boil, then reduce the heat to a low simmer and cook, covered, for 20 minutes.

Stir and cook, uncovered, for 8 to 10 minutes more, or until the stew has thickened and the vegetables are fork-tender. Stir in the lemon juice and season with salt and freshly ground black pepper.

Make the lemon couscous: Bring a medium pot of salted water to a boil. Add the couscous and cook until al dente, 7 to 8 minutes. Drain, let cool slightly, then transfer to a serving bowl, and toss with the olive oil, lemon juice, lemon zest, parsley, and salt and black pepper to taste. Fluff with a fork.

Serve the vegetable tagine over the lemon couscous and garnish with the chopped parsley and sliced almonds. Serve with lemon wedges and harissa, if desired.

SERVES 4 **VEGAN** **GLUTEN-FREE:** Use quinoa in place of the couscous.

CHARRED CAULIFLOWER PITAS WITH HALLOUMI & HARISSA

This recipe is one of our go-to weeknight dinners, especially if I have Homemade Harissa (page 281) in the fridge. The harissa keeps for at least a week—have it on hand to whip up this quick, flavorful dinner. Just roast the cauliflower and halloumi until well charred, and stuff everything into a warm pita with spicy arugula.

---

1 small cauliflower, sliced into 1-inch-thick slabs

Extra-virgin olive oil, for drizzling

Sea salt and freshly ground black pepper

8 ounces halloumi cheese, sliced widthwise into ¼-inch-thick pieces

2 large or 4 smaller pitas

½ cup Homemade Harissa (page 281)

2 cups arugula

Preheat the broiler and line one large baking sheet and one small baking sheet with foil. Spray with cooking spray.

Rub the cauliflower slabs with olive oil, salt, and pepper on both sides and arrange them on the large baking sheet. Broil until very charred and tender, turning once. I broil mine for 13 minutes on one side and 5 on the other, but time will vary widely among broilers.

Place the halloumi slices on the smaller baking sheet and broil for 4 minutes per side, or until dark brown around the edges.

Turn off the broiler and warm the pitas in the oven for 1 minute.

Slice the pitas in half and assemble with a generous slather of the harissa, the arugula, the broiled halloumi, and the charred cauliflower. Serve with extra harissa on the side.

SERVES 4

JAPANESE UDON HOT POT FOR TWO

I don't have an Instant Pot®, a Crock-Pot®, or whatever kind of pot that's currently on trend, but I love cooking this recipe in a humble no-tech Japanese clay pot on the stove. It's a fun date-night-in recipe, especially if your date loves mushrooms and udon as much as mine does. The broth is earthy and healing from the mushrooms, kombu, and ginger. This is not a spicy, punch-you-in-the-face-with-bold-flavor type of recipe. Instead it reminds me of some of the simple, lovely meals we've eaten in Japan, where the focus is on the clean taste of each ingredient. This recipe can also be made in a standard-sized saucepan.

4 cups water

1 (4-inch) strip kombu*

2½ tablespoons tamari, plus more for serving

2½ tablespoons rice vinegar

½ teaspoon grated fresh ginger

½ garlic clove, minced

6 ounces mixed mushrooms, such as enoki and shiitake, larger mushrooms stemmed and sliced

¼ sweet potato, sliced into ¼-inch half moons

4 ounces fresh jumbo udon noodles* or dried udon

2 ounces baby bok choy, sliced into bite-size wedges

1 scallion, chopped

2 ounces extra-firm tofu, sliced, or 2 Soft-Boiled Eggs (page 60)

½ nori sheet, cut into matchsticks with scissors (optional)

1 teaspoon sesame seeds (optional)

*Find these ingredients in the Asian section of grocery stores or at any Asian market.

In a donabe or a 3-quart saucepan, combine the water and the kombu. Simmer very gently for 10 minutes. Don't boil, or the kombu will cause the broth to become bitter. Remove and discard the kombu. Add the tamari, rice vinegar, ginger, garlic, mushrooms, and sweet potato. Bring to a boil, cover, and then reduce the heat and simmer for 15 minutes. The mushrooms should be soft and the sweet potato tender.

Bring a large pot of water to a boil. Prepare the noodles according to the package directions. Drain and rinse under cold running water.

Add the noodles, bok choy, scallion, and tofu to the pot. Cover and allow the bok choy to steam for a minute or two, until tender but still bright green.

Serve the soup with the nori, sesame seeds, if desired, and additional tamari.

SERVES 2   VEGAN   GLUTEN-FREE: Use gluten-free noodles.

Pasta

[FIVE EASY FAVORITES]

EACH RECIPE SERVES 2

1 SUMMER THYME PASTA

Heat **2 tablespoons olive oil** in a medium skillet over low heat. Add **⅓ cup chopped shallot**; **3 cups cherry tomatoes**; leaves of **6 sprigs fresh thyme**; and pinches of **salt, pepper,** and **red pepper flakes**. Sauté until the tomatoes are bursting, about 6 minutes, then add **½ teaspoon balsamic vinegar** and **2 minced garlic cloves**. Stir in **4 ounces cooked orecchiette**. Top with shaved **pecorino cheese** and **fresh basil**.

2 ZUCCHINI CARBONARA

In a small bowl, beat **1 egg** with **2 tablespoons almond milk** and **¼ cup grated pecorino cheese**. Heat **½ tablespoon olive oil** in a medium skillet over medium heat. Add thinly sliced strips of **1 zucchini** and pinches of **salt** and **pepper**. Sauté until soft, then remove from the heat. Add **4 ounces cooked bucatini** and the egg mixture and toss. Top with **fresh basil**.

TIP For well-seasoned pasta, heavily salt your pasta cooking water.

3
LEMON AGLIO OLIO WITH KALE

Heat **1 tablespoon olive oil** in a skillet over low heat. Add **¼ teaspoon red pepper flakes**, **1 minced garlic clove**, **4 cups chopped lacinato kale**, **salt**, and **pepper**. Toss with **6 ounces cooked spaghetti** and **2 tablespoons lemon juice**. Top with diced **Quick Preserved Lemons** (page 279) or **lemon zest**, toasted **pine nuts**, and shaved **pecorino cheese**.

Season to taste with salt and pepper before serving!

FENNEL FETTUCINE ## 4

Slice **one fennel bulb** into wedges and roast until tender (page 235). Mix **⅓ cup vegan Caesar dressing** (page 111) with **¼ cup pasta cooking water** and toss with **4 ounces cooked fettuccine**. Top with the fennel wedges, **¼ cup peas**, chopped **chives**, **tarragon**, **salt**, and **pepper**. Serve with **lemon wedges**.

5
ROASTED CAULIFLOWER PASTA WITH YOGURT & HARISSA

Toss **4 ounces cooked pasta** with **2 cups roasted cauliflower** (page 235). Drizzle with **olive oil**, and top with **Homemade Harissa** (page 281), **Greek yogurt**, **roasted chickpeas** (page 293), **red pepper flakes**, **mint**, and **microgreens** or **arugula**.

SI
DIS

SIDE DISHES

SWEET POTATO WEDGES WITH FARRO & TAHINI

Some ingredients are just meant to be together: tomatoes and basil, peanut butter and jelly, and lemon and lavender, for example, are matches made in heaven. I'd like to add sweet potatoes and tahini to that mix. These cozy sweet potato wedges drizzled with bright, creamy lemon tahini dressing create a flavor pairing that is far more than the sum of its parts. Serve over the herbed farro and arugula for a hearty side dish or delicious lunch.

1 medium sweet potato, halved lengthwise and cut into 12 wedges

Extra-virgin olive oil, for drizzling

Sea salt and freshly ground black pepper

Lemon Tahini Dressing (page 130)

Red pepper flakes (optional)

Herbed Farro

2 cups cooked farro or soft wheat berries (page 22)

2 teaspoons extra-virgin olive oil

¼ teaspoon sea salt, plus more to taste

1 tablespoon fresh lemon juice, plus lemon wedges for serving

⅓ cup chopped fresh parsley

⅓ cup chopped fresh cilantro

2 tablespoons chopped chives

Pinch of cayenne pepper

2 cups baby arugula

Freshly ground black pepper

Preheat the oven to 425°F and line a baking sheet with parchment paper. Place the sweet potato wedges on the baking sheet, drizzle with olive oil, and season with pinches of salt and a few grinds of black pepper. Toss to coat, then spread the wedges on the baking sheet with a little space between each one. Roast for 25 to 30 minutes, or until golden brown around the edges.

Make the farro: In a large bowl, toss the farro with the olive oil, salt, lemon juice, parsley, cilantro, chives, cayenne, arugula, and a few grinds of black pepper.

Arrange the farro salad on a platter and top with the roasted sweet potatoes. Drizzle with the tahini dressing. Serve with lemon wedges and red pepper flakes, if desired.

SERVES 4 | VEGAN | GLUTEN-FREE: Use quinoa in place of the farro.

GRILLED RADISHES WITH CHICKPEAS & RADISH-GREEN GODDESS

If you think you don't love radishes, don't turn the page! The grill gives them a nice char, sweetening their bitter flavor. If the grilled radishes aren't enough to turn you into a radish fan on their own, try them with the fresh radish-green-herb sauce. It's bright and creamy, playing with the grilled radishes and lemony marinated chickpeas to make a lovely spring side or light dinner.

❖

Radish–Green Goddess

1 cup loose-packed radish greens

1 garlic clove

⅓ cup loose-packed basil, chopped

½ teaspoon lemon zest

1 tablespoon lemon juice

½ teaspoon honey or maple syrup

Heaping ½ teaspoon sea salt

¾ cup whole milk Greek yogurt

2 tablespoons extra-virgin olive oil

Radishes and Chickpeas

8 radishes

Extra-virgin olive oil, for drizzling

Sea salt and freshly ground black pepper

1 recipe Marinated Chickpeas (page 293)

2 Persian cucumbers, thinly sliced

2 tablespoons finely chopped parsley

2 tablespoons toasted pine nuts

Flaky sea salt, for sprinkling

Note: *Extra sauce can be stored in the fridge and used for dipping veggies or as a sandwich spread.*

Make the radish-green goddess: Bring a small pot of water to a boil and set a bowl of ice water nearby. Drop the greens and garlic into the boiling water to blanch. Remove the greens after about 10 seconds, or until just wilted, and transfer to the ice water. Remove the garlic 1 minute later and set aside. Drain the greens, pat dry, and chop.

In a food processor, place the radish greens, garlic, basil, lemon zest, lemon juice, honey, salt, and yogurt. Pulse until well combined. Drizzle in the olive oil and pulse again. Chill until ready to use.

Preheat a grill to medium-high. Thinly slice 2 radishes and set aside. Drizzle the remaining 6 whole radishes with olive oil, salt, and pepper and grill 3 minutes per side, or until charred around the edges. Slice any large radishes in quarters and small ones in half.

Assemble the dish with the marinated chickpeas, cucumbers, sliced raw radishes, and parsley and toss gently. Add the grilled radishes, pine nuts, drizzles of olive oil, sprinkles of flaky sea salt, and dollops of yogurt sauce. Serve with remaining sauce on the side.

SERVES 4

GLUTEN-FREE

TIP Turn any leftovers into grainless bowl meals. Add Sriracha Tofu (page 147) and steamed spinach to individual servings.

ORANGE-SCENTED CAULIFLOWER RICE PILAF

This is my take on a jeweled rice pilaf that uses cauliflower "rice" instead of regular rice. The dressing is tangy, slightly sweet, and just a tad spicy. The toasted nuts, the currants, and the pop of pomegranate and mint in the pilaf bring so many flavors and textures to this dish. Serve this as a side dish with any type of protein you enjoy.

Dressing

1 tablespoon orange zest

3 tablespoons fresh-squeezed orange juice

½ tablespoon extra-virgin olive oil

1 tablespoon rice vinegar

1 teaspoon minced fresh ginger

½ teaspoon sriracha

½ teaspoon sea salt

Pinch of red pepper flakes

Pilaf

1 small cauliflower, trimmed and cut into florets (1 pound)

½ tablespoon extra-virgin olive oil

1 shallot, chopped (⅓ cup)

2 scallions, finely sliced

Sea salt and freshly ground black pepper

¼ cup toasted chopped almonds

¼ cup toasted chopped pistachios

¼ cup dried currants

¼ cup pomegranate seeds

⅓ cup chopped fresh parsley

⅓ cup chopped fresh cilantro

¼ cup fresh mint leaves

1½ teaspoons orange zest

Orange wedges, for serving

Make the dressing: In a small bowl, whisk together the orange zest, orange juice, olive oil, rice vinegar, ginger, sriracha, salt, and red pepper flakes. Set aside.

Make the pilaf: Working in several batches, place the cauliflower in a food processor and pulse until it resembles rice. This should yield about 4 cups riced cauliflower.

Heat the olive oil in a large skillet over medium heat. Add the shallot and cook, stirring, for 6 minutes or until soft. Add the cauliflower rice, scallions, a generous pinch of salt, and a few grinds of black pepper. Cook, stirring frequently, for 2 to 3 minutes more, until the cauliflower has just softened. Do not overcook.

Remove the skillet from the heat and let it cool slightly. Transfer to a large bowl and toss with three-quarters of the dressing, the almonds, pistachios, currants, pomegranate seeds, parsley, cilantro, mint, and orange zest. Season to taste with salt and pepper.

Transfer to a platter, drizzle with the remaining dressing, and serve with the orange wedges.

SERVES 4

VEGAN & GLUTEN-FREE

TAHINI COLLARD GREEN SLAW

I have to thank the Whole Foods salad bar for this idea. I thought I had slawed every type of vegetable possible, until one day I discovered collard green slaw—genius! I came home to re-create my own version while the taste was still fresh in my memory. Raw collard greens are sturdy enough to be slathered in a thick, creamy dressing. This one is made with tahini instead of mayo. Slice your collards super thin by first rolling them, then slicing into a chiffonade.

Dressing

¼ cup tahini

3 tablespoons fresh orange juice

2 tablespoons fresh lemon juice

2 tablespoons apple cider vinegar

1 tablespoon Dijon mustard

½ teaspoon sea salt

¼ teaspoon freshly ground black pepper

Slaw

1 bunch collard greens

2 cups shredded red cabbage

2 cups shredded carrots

1 heaping cup snap peas, halved lengthwise and widthwise

3 scallions, sliced

¼ cup sesame seeds

Make the dressing: In a small bowl, stir together the tahini, orange juice, lemon juice, apple cider vinegar, mustard, salt, and pepper. Set aside.

Make the slaw: Remove the coarse stems that run down the center of the collard greens. Stack the collard leaves on top of one another, roll them up lengthwise, and slice into thin shreds. In a large bowl, combine the collard greens, cabbage, carrots, snap peas, and scallions and toss.

Drizzle the dressing over the vegetables and toss to coat. The slaw is best if you let it sit at room temperature for at least 10 minutes before serving. Taste and adjust seasonings. Top with the sesame seeds.

SERVES 4 TO 6   VEGAN & GLUTEN-FREE

TIP This slaw not only keeps well in the fridge for a few days but also gets better on days 2 and 3, when the collards have softened.

VEGAN CAULIFLOWER GRATIN

Once fall hits, I crave creamy, cozy foods, which is why I'm pretty obsessed with this cauliflower side dish. Instead of cheese and heavy cream, the "cream" sauce here is made by chopping and blending the core of the cauliflower with cashews, a little lemon juice, and a touch of Dijon mustard (which you won't really taste, but it adds a necessary tang). I love serving this one as part of a holiday dinner.

---

1 small cauliflower (1 pound)

½ cup raw cashews

¾ cup water

2 tablespoons fresh lemon juice

1 tablespoon miso paste

3 garlic cloves

½ teaspoon Dijon mustard

3 tablespoons extra-virgin olive oil, plus more for brushing

½ teaspoon sea salt, plus more to taste

Freshly ground black pepper

1 small yellow onion, thinly sliced

Topping

¼ cup panko bread crumbs

¼ cup crushed pine nuts or hemp seeds

¼ teaspoon sea salt

¼ cup finely chopped fresh parsley

Preheat the oven to 400°F and brush an 11×7-inch baking dish with olive oil.

Break the cauliflower florets into small bite-sized pieces and set aside for later use.

Roughly chop the cauliflower cores. Bring a medium pot of salted water to a boil and boil the cauliflower cores (not the florets!) for 5 minutes or until fork-tender. Transfer to a blender along with the cashews, water, lemon juice, miso paste, garlic, mustard, 2 tablespoons of the olive oil, the salt, and several grinds of black pepper. Blend until creamy.

Make the topping: In a small bowl, mix together the panko, pine nuts, and sea salt. Set aside.

Heat the remaining 1 tablespoon olive oil in a large skillet over medium heat. Add the onion and pinches of salt and sauté until softened, about 5 minutes. Stir in the cauliflower florets and half of the sauce. Toss to combine and transfer to the baking dish. Evenly pour the remaining sauce on top and sprinkle with the panko mixture. Bake for 30 minutes or until the cauliflower is golden brown and tender. Top with the parsley and serve.

SERVES 6

VEGAN GLUTEN-FREE: Use gluten-free panko.

TIP See my Fall Harvest Feast menu suggestions on page 307.

ROASTED CARROTS WITH CARROT TOP TZATZIKI

Don't toss those carrot tops! I love finding creative uses for them—I'll make them into chimichurri, pesto, or simply chop them and sprinkle them into my salads. In this recipe, I swirl them into a nontraditional tzatziki that's so delicious with these spiced roasted carrots. Save this recipe for the day you have a beautiful, fresh bunch of carrots with lush tops. Make sure to get smaller, fresh carrots, as they're sweeter and more concentrated in flavor, which makes all the difference in this simple recipe.

1 bunch carrots with green tops, scrubbed and trimmed, tops reserved for sauce

Extra-virgin olive oil, for drizzling

Heaping ¼ teaspoon ground cumin

Heaping ¼ teaspoon ground coriander

Sea salt and freshly ground black pepper

Carrot Top Tzatziki

½ cup whole milk Greek yogurt

1 tablespoon extra-virgin olive oil

1 garlic clove, minced

¼ teaspoon lemon zest

1½ tablespoons fresh lemon juice

¼ cup chopped carrot tops, half reserved for garnish

2 tablespoons chopped fresh mint leaves, half reserved for garnish

2 tablespoons chopped fresh dill, half reserved for garnish

2 tablespoons water

¼ teaspoon sea salt

Freshly ground black pepper

Preheat the oven to 425°F and line a baking sheet with parchment paper.

Place the carrots whole on the baking sheet and toss with a drizzle of olive oil, the cumin, coriander, and pinches of salt and pepper. Roll the carrots with your hands to coat and arrange them on the sheet with space between the carrots. Roast for 15 to 25 minutes, or until the carrots are fork-tender and lightly browned but not mushy. The timing will depend on the size of your carrots. Remove from the oven and slice in half lengthwise.

Make the carrot top tzatziki: In a small bowl, mix together the yogurt, olive oil, garlic, lemon zest, lemon juice, 2 tablespoons carrot tops, 1 tablespoon mint, 1 tablespoon dill, the water, salt, and a few grinds of black pepper.

Spread the tzatziki sauce onto a platter. Arrange the carrots on top of the sauce. Garnish with the reserved carrot tops, mint, and dill. Season to taste, as desired.

SERVES 4

GLUTEN-FREE

TIP   Make a meal out of any leftover carrots by chopping and tossing them over farro with roasted chickpeas, arugula, toasted nuts or seeds, feta cheese, and dollops of extra tzatziki sauce.

ROSEMARY & MEYER LEMON FOCACCIA

One winter during his holiday work break, Jack took up bread baking. While it was a fun and delicious time, the multi-rise rustic loaves he made were time consuming! Foccacia, on the other hand, doesn't require a weekend of bread babysitting. I particularly love this recipe, with its pop of Meyer lemon. Make sure you get thin-skinned organic Meyer lemons and slice them as thinly as you can so that the rind is tender enough to enjoy.

❖

1¾ cups warm water (105° to 115°F)

1 (¼-ounce) package active dry yeast

1 tablespoon cane sugar

3½ cups all-purpose flour, plus more for kneading

1½ cups whole wheat flour

1 tablespoon sea salt

½ cup extra-virgin olive oil, plus more for brushing

2 small thin-skinned Meyer lemons, very thinly sliced and seeded

1 tablespoon minced rosemary

½ teaspoon red pepper flakes

Flaky sea salt, for sprinkling

In a medium bowl, stir together the water, yeast, and sugar. Set aside for 5 minutes, until the yeast is foamy.

In the bowl of a mixer fitted with a dough hook attachment, place the flours, salt, ¼ cup of the olive oil, and the yeast mixture and mix on medium speed until the dough forms a ball around the hook, 5 to 6 minutes.

Turn the dough onto a lightly floured surface and knead several times, sprinkling with more flour, as needed, and form into a ball. Brush a large bowl with olive oil, and place the dough inside. Cover with plastic wrap and set aside to rise until doubled in size, 40 to 50 minutes.

Coat a 10×15-inch rimmed baking sheet with the remaining ¼ cup olive oil. Punch the dough down, transfer to a lightly floured surface, and knead several times. Place the dough in the pan and press to spread it out to the pan's edges. Flip the dough over and spread it to the edges again. Make indentations with your fingers, every few inches apart, all over the dough. Cover the baking sheet with plastic wrap and allow the dough to rise until it has doubled in size, about 40 minutes.

Preheat the oven to 425°F. Remove the plastic wrap and scatter the lemon slices over the surface of the dough. Sprinkle with the rosemary, red pepper flakes, and flaky salt and bake for 20 minutes, until golden brown.

SERVES 6 TO 8   VEGAN

BROCCOLI RABE & BURRATA WITH LEMON

I love a simple vegetable side that's . . . well . . . simple. If you have preserved lemons at the ready, this recipe takes roughly ten minutes from start to finish. Broccoli rabe is a wonderful bitter green that becomes less bitter the longer it cooks, which is why I blanch, then sauté it with olive oil, garlic, and red pepper flakes. Creamy burrata, tangy lemons, and toasty pistachios give this simple dish plenty of contrasting flavors and textures. Jack and I often pass some bread and wine and call this (a light) dinner.

***

1 bunch broccoli rabe, tips of stems trimmed off

1 to 2 tablespoons extra-virgin olive oil, plus more for drizzling

2 garlic cloves, sliced

¼ teaspoon red pepper flakes

4 ounces burrata or fresh mozzarella

1 tablespoon chopped Quick Preserved Lemons (page 279) or ½ tablespoon fresh lemon juice

2 tablespoons crushed toasted pistachios

Flaky sea salt, for sprinkling

Bring a large pot of salted water to a boil. Boil the broccoli rabe for 3 minutes, then drain.

In a large, deep skillet over medium heat, heat enough olive oil to nicely coat the bottom of the pan, 1 to 2 tablespoons. Stir in the garlic and cook for 30 seconds, then stir in the red pepper flakes. Add the broccoli rabe and sauté, shaking the pan and gently tossing so that it cooks evenly, until tender, especially the stems, for 3 to 5 minutes.

Remove from the pan and drain off any excess liquid. Arrange the broccoli on a plate or platter. Tear the burrata and place evenly spaced pieces among the broccoli rabe. Sprinkle with the preserved lemons, pistachios, and flaky sea salt. Drizzle with olive oil, if desired, and serve.

SERVES 4

VEGAN: Skip the burrata and add dollops of the Almond Cheese on page 73.

GLUTEN-FREE

ROASTING VEGETABLES

— FROM A TO Z —

TIP Toss roasted veggies into grain bowls and salads with dressings from page 130.

To peel or not to peel? Unless otherwise listed, I typically don't peel! Great nutrients are in those skins. If dirty: scrub. If grubby: then peel.

Preheat the oven and line a baking sheet with parchment paper.
Toss the vegetables with olive oil, sea salt, and pepper and arrange
evenly on the sheet. Roast until golden brown around the edges.
Times may vary based on size and freshness of the vegetables.

PRODUCE	TEMP	PREP INSTRUCTIONS	MINUTES
ACORN SQUASH	425°F	scoop out seeds, cut into 2-inch wedges	40 to 55
ASPARAGUS	425°F	trim woody ends, roast whole	12
BEETS	425°F	wrap in foil with olive oil, salt, and pepper (peel after roasting)	60
BELL PEPPERS	425°F	roast whole and dry (stem and peel after roasting)	20 to 30
BROCCOLI	400°F	break into florets	15 to 20
BRUSSELS SPROUTS	425°F	slice in half	25 to 35
BUTTERNUT SQUASH	400°F	peel, scoop out seeds, dice	30 to 35
CARROTS	450°F	roast whole or cut into 1-inch pieces	15 to 25
CAULIFLOWER	425°F	break into florets	25 to 30
DELICATA SQUASH	425°F	slice in half, scoop out seeds, slice into 1-inch pieces	20 to 30
EGGPLANT	425°F	cut into 1-inch dice	20 to 25
FENNEL	400°F	remove tops, slice into 1-inch wedges	25 to 35
GARLIC	375°F	slice off the top of the head, wrap in foil	35 to 40
JALAPEÑO PEPPERS	450°F	roast whole and dry (stem and peel after roasting)	15
KABOCHA SQUASH	425°F	scoop out seeds, slice into wedges	40 to 55
KOHLRABI	425°F	cut into 1-inch dice	30 to 35
LEEKS	425°F	chop into 1-inch pieces, rinse well	15 to 20
MUSHROOMS (CREMINI)	425°F	large ones chopped into 1-inch pieces, small ones left whole	15
ONIONS	425°F	slice into 1-inch wedges	30
PARSNIPS	425°F	chop into 1-inch pieces	20 to 25
POBLANO PEPPERS	425°F	roast whole and dry (stem and peel after roasting)	20 to 30
POTATOES	425°F	slice small ones in half, slice larger ones into 1-inch wedges	30 to 35
RADICCHIO	425°F	cut into 6 or 8 wedges, flip mid-roast	15 to 20
RADISHES (RED)	450°F	slice in half, roast cut-side down	10 to 12
RUTABAGA	425°F	chop into 1-inch pieces	35 to 40
SHALLOTS	400°F	peel, cut large ones in half, toss mid-roast	30 to 40
SPAGHETTI SQUASH	400°F	cut in half, scoop out seeds, roast cut-side down, fluff with fork	30 to 40
SWEET POTATOES	425°F	roast whole (no foil) or cut into 1-inch pieces	25 to 60
TOMATOES (CHERRY)	300°F	slice in half, place cut-side up.	60 to 90
TURNIPS	450°F	chop into 1-inch pieces	25 to 30
YELLOW SQUASH	425°F	cut into ½-inch rounds	8 to 10
ZUCCHINI	425°F	cut into ½-inch rounds	8 to 10

VEGETABLES

VEGETABLE PREP

Unless otherwise specified, drizzle vegetables with olive oil and sprinkle with sea salt and black pepper before grilling. Grill on medium-high heat until char marks form. Every grill is different, so times will vary. To keep vegetables from sticking to the grill, wait until the grill is fully preheated. Use cooking spray on the grill, if desired.

ASPARAGUS	Grill whole spears for 3 to 4 minutes per side, or until tender but still crisp and charred. Squeeze with lemon.
AVOCADOS	Grill halves, cut-side down, for 3 to 5 minutes, or until char marks form. Serve with a squeeze of lime and a sprinkle of salt.
BROCCOLI	Cut into large florets and grill for 3 to 4 minutes per side, until charred and tender. Drizzle with lemon juice and sprinkle with Parmesan cheese.
CAULIFLOWER	Grill 1-inch-thick steaks for 5 to 7 minutes per side, until charred. Use in place of the roasted steaks in the Cauliflower Steaks with Lemon Salsa Verde (page 145). Grill cauliflower florets for 3 to 5 minutes per side.
CORN	Place corn cobs on the grill and rotate every few minutes until charred all over. Serve on the cob with a squeeze of lime, or slice kernels off and toss them into a summer salad.
EGGPLANT	Slice small eggplants in half and grill each side for 5 to 8 minutes, or until tender and charred. Slice larger eggplants into planks or rounds and grill for 3 to 4 minutes per side. Grill larger eggplants to stuff (see Mediterranean Stuffed Eggplant, page 179).
LEEKS	Slice leeks in half lengthwise. Rinse and dry well. Grill each side until charred and tender. Squeeze with lemon and serve, or chop and add to salads.
MUSHROOMS	Coat mushrooms with olive oil, tamari, and balsamic vinegar. Grill portobello caps for 5 to 7 minutes per side, and shiitake and cremini caps for 2 to 3 minutes per side. Or skewer cremini mushrooms and grill for 8 minutes per side, or until nicely charred.
OKRA	Skewer and grill for 3 to 5 minutes per side, until charred and tender. Serve with Chimichurri (page 283).
ONIONS	Cut red onions into wedges, skewer, and grill for 8 minutes per side. These add flavor and color to skewers with other veggies!
PEACHES	Spray grill well. Slice peaches into wedges and grill for 2 to 3 minutes per side.
PEPPERS	Grill peppers whole by placing them dry on the grill, and rotate until heavily charred all over. Place in a bowl, cover with foil, and set aside for 15 minutes. When cool to the touch, remove the stem and ribbing and some of the black char. Use in any recipe that calls for a roasted red pepper (Homemade Harissa, page 281). Grill bell peppers or poblano peppers to stuff (Spicy Black Bean & Mango Stuffed Peppers, page 165), or skewer pepper chunks (Rainbow Summer Veggie Skewers, page 163).
(fingerling and new potatoes) **POTATOES**	Parboil until fork-tender. Slice in half. Toss generously with olive oil, salt, and pepper. Grill cut-side down until charred, then flip. The timing will depend on the size of your potatoes.
RADICCHIO	Slice into quarters and grill each side. Drizzle with balsamic vinegar and sprinkle with shaved pecorino cheese.
ROMAINE LETTUCE	Slice in half and grill for 1 to 2 minutes per side. See Grilled Romaine Vegan Caesar Wedges (page 111).
SHISHITO PEPPERS	Use a grill grate, grill pan, or foil. Grill until well blistered. Drizzle with sesame oil and sprinkle with sesame seeds.
SUMMER SQUASH	Cut into planks and grill for 2 to 4 minutes per side, or cut into rounds, skewer, and grill for 8 minutes per side. See Rainbow Summer Veggie Skewers (page 163).
TOMATOES	Grill whole cherry tomatoes until blistered. Tomatoes on the vine or Roma tomatoes, grill 12 to 15 minutes or until bursting.

DESS

ERTS

FLOURLESS ALMOND CHOCOLATE CHIP COOKIES

When I first started working on this recipe, I was trying a temporary elimination diet where I wasn't eating dairy or grains. I was doing okay skipping out on sweets, until one day I wasn't—and I NEEDED a cookie. So I came up with this recipe, which let me have my cookie and eat it too. I've been tweaking this recipe ever since. Not only does everyone love this cookie, regardless of any dietary restrictions, but it's also now a one-bowl recipe! Almonds give the cookies a rich consistency and nutty flavor, and while I've listed the flaky sea salt on top of the cookies as optional, I highly recommend it because it really takes these over the top.

1 tablespoon ground flaxseed

3 tablespoons water, plus more if necessary

2 tablespoons coconut oil, softened but not melted

½ cup coconut sugar or brown sugar

¼ cup almond butter

1 teaspoon vanilla extract

2 cups almond flour

½ teaspoon baking soda

¼ teaspoon sea salt

½ cup semisweet chocolate chips

Flaky sea salt, for sprinkling (optional)

Preheat the oven to 350°F and line a baking sheet with parchment paper.

In the bottom of a large bowl, whisk together the ground flaxseed and water and let thicken for 5 minutes.

To the same bowl, add the coconut oil, coconut sugar, almond butter, and vanilla. Whisk until well combined. Add the almond flour and sprinkle the baking soda and salt evenly over the mixture. Use a spatula or wooden spoon to stir until well combined, adding 1 to 2 tablespoons water if the mixture is too dry. Fold in the chocolate chips.

Use a 2-tablespoon cookie scoop to scoop the dough onto the baking sheet. Press each ball down slightly and sprinkle with flaky sea salt, if using. Bake for 10 to 13 minutes or until the edges are just starting to brown.

Cool on the pan for 5 minutes and then transfer to a wire rack to finish cooling.

When the cookies are completely cool, they can be stored in an airtight container or frozen.

Note: *To reheat frozen cookies, bake in a 350°F oven for 5 minutes, or until warmed through.*

MAKES 16 COOKIES

VEGAN & GLUTEN-FREE

LEMON OLIVE OIL PISTACHIO CAKE

How could a book titled *Love & Lemons* not have a lemon cake recipe? That's what I asked myself after our first book, so this recipe is here to remedy the situation. Pistachio flour made from grinding pistachios in the blender gives this cake a wonderful nutty flavor and substantial texture. Don't skip the glaze on top because that's what gives this cake its bright, zesty flavor. Almond flour also works here in place of the pistachio flour. This recipe works as mini cakes or as a standard-size loaf.

---

1 cup shelled raw pistachios*

1 cup all-purpose flour

1 teaspoon baking powder

½ teaspoon sea salt

⅓ cup extra-virgin olive oil

⅓ cup almond milk

¾ cup cane sugar

3 large eggs

1 tablespoon lemon zest

3 tablespoons fresh lemon juice

1 tablespoon chopped pistachios, for garnish

Glaze

1 cup powdered sugar

1 tablespoon lemon zest

2 to 3 tablespoons fresh lemon juice

Can be substituted with 1 cup almond flour.

Preheat the oven to 350°F and lightly spray 2 (6-inch) mini cake pans or 1 loaf pan.

Process the pistachios in a blender to produce a coarse meal or flour. Measure 1 cup of pistachio flour.

In a medium bowl, whisk together the 1 cup of pistachio flour, the all-purpose flour, baking powder, and salt.

In a large bowl, combine the olive oil, almond milk, sugar, eggs, lemon zest, and lemon juice. Whisk vigorously until frothy. Fold in the dry ingredients and mix until just combined.

Pour the batter into the prepared pans and bake until a toothpick inserted in the middle comes out clean, about 35 minutes for mini cakes and 45 minutes for a loaf. Let cool for 10 minutes, then remove from the pan and cool completely on a wire rack.

Make the glaze: In a medium bowl, combine the powdered sugar, lemon zest, and lemon juice as needed to make a smooth, pourable glaze. Drizzle over the cooled cake and garnish with the chopped pistachios.

SERVES 8

VEGAN DATE BROWNIES

I love a brownie that's fudgy in the middle with a bit of a crisp, craggly-edged crust. For a long time, my attempts at making brownies vegan ended up more like soft chocolate cake than brownies. My mom finally cracked the code one day by blending the secret ingredient—dates!—into the batter. It not only sweetens these naturally but creates a decadent texture. Don't skip the chocolate chips (or chocolate chunks), as they contribute to the inner fudginess.

---

6 large Medjool dates, pitted

½ cup Homemade Oat Flour (page 61)

⅓ cup unsweetened cocoa powder

1½ teaspoons baking soda

⅛ teaspoon sea salt

1¼ cups creamy cashew butter

½ cup plus 2 tablespoons maple syrup

1 teaspoon vanilla extract

½ cup raspberries

⅓ cup dark chocolate chips

⅓ cup chopped macadamia nuts

Flaky sea salt, for sprinkling (optional)

Preheat the oven to 325°F. Lightly spray an 8×8-inch baking pan with nonstick cooking spray and then line the pan with parchment paper, leaving a few inches of overhang on two sides.

If your dates are not soft, soak them in a small bowl of warm water for 5 to 10 minutes.

In a medium bowl, stir together the oat flour, cocoa powder, baking soda, and salt.

In a food processor, place the cashew butter, maple syrup, vanilla, and the soft dates. Process until well combined. Scoop the mixture into the bowl of dry ingredients and fold until all the dry ingredients are incorporated. The mixture will form a sticky ball.

Use your fingertips to gently spread the batter to the edges of the pan, forming a thicker crust around the edges. Be careful not to overwork the batter or press down too firmly. Sprinkle with the raspberries, chocolate chips, macadamia nuts, and flaky sea salt, if using.

Bake for 20 minutes, or until the edges are slightly firm and pulling away from the pan but the center is still moist. Let cool completely before slicing into squares.

MAKES 16 BROWNIES

VEGAN & GLUTEN-FREE

CREAMY VEGAN LEMON BARS

These decadent bars fill my craving for a creamy dessert, but without cream! The filling of these is rich from blending raw cashews and coconut cream, and they're very tangy, thanks to my love of lemon. These are best stored in the freezer. I like to freeze them until they set, and slice them into bars so that later I can thaw one at a time for an individual serving.

Crust

9 soft Medjool dates, pitted

1 cup walnuts

¾ cup gluten-free whole rolled oats

Heaping ¼ teaspoon sea salt

1 to 2 tablespoons water

Filling

1 (14-ounce) can coconut cream*

1¼ cups raw cashews

2 tablespoons lemon zest

⅓ cup fresh lemon juice

⅓ cup maple syrup

⅛ teaspoon sea salt

Be sure to use coconut cream as opposed to coconut milk.

Make the crust: In a food processor, place the dates, walnuts, oats, and salt and process until the mixture comes together into a sticky ball. If necessary, gradually add 1 to 2 tablespoons of water.

Line a 7×9-inch or 8×8-inch baking pan with parchment paper and press the crust to the edges of the pan. The crust is very sticky, so I like to use a sheet of parchment paper on top to help smooth it out. Place the pan in the freezer while you make the filling.

Make the filling: In a high-speed blender, puree the coconut cream, cashews, lemon zest, lemon juice, maple syrup, and salt until smooth. Pour the filling over the crust and freeze overnight. Let thaw at room temperature for 20 minutes before slicing into bars and serving.

MAKES 16 BARS

VEGAN & GLUTEN-FREE

LEMON LAVENDER SHORTBREAD COOKIES

What's more Love & Lemons than lemon heart-shaped cookies? Flecks of lavender bring out the lemon flavor in these lightly sweet treats. If you can't find dried lavender, fresh rosemary and thyme are lovely here as well. Enjoy these cookies with a cup of your favorite tea.

❖

½ cup unsalted butter, softened

⅓ cup cane sugar

Zest of 1 medium lemon

1 tablespoon fresh lemon juice

1 teaspoon dried lavender

1¼ cups all-purpose flour, plus more for rolling

¼ teaspoon sea salt

Preheat the oven to 350°F and line a large baking sheet with parchment paper.

In the bowl of an electric mixer, cream the butter. Add the sugar and beat until fluffy, scraping down the sides of the bowl as needed. Add the lemon zest, lemon juice, and lavender and mix again. Add the flour and salt and mix until just combined. Turn the dough out onto a floured surface and flatten into a 1-inch disk. If the dough is sticky, wrap and chill for 15 to 30 minutes until firm but still pliable.

Roll the dough on a lightly floured surface until about ¼ inch thick. If desired, the dough can be rolled between two pieces of parchment paper. Use 2-inch cookie cutters to cut out desired shapes. Transfer to the baking sheet and bake for 10 to 14 minutes, or until the edges are lightly browned.

Remove from the oven and transfer the cookies to wire racks to cool. Store at room temperature for up to 5 days.

MAKES *30* COOKIES

PEANUT BUTTER SNICKERDOODLES

I love snickerdoodles, but I always wanted to make a great version without using so much butter . . . then I had the idea to try incorporating peanut butter! These delicious soft little cookies are fun to mix together and roll out. If there are extras, they freeze well.

❖

1 tablespoon ground flaxseed

3 tablespoons water

1½ cups all-purpose flour

1 cup Homemade Oat Flour (page 61)

1 teaspoon baking powder

½ teaspoon baking soda

¼ teaspoon sea salt

1 cup maple syrup

½ cup coconut oil, softened but not melted

½ cup natural creamy peanut butter

1 teaspoon vanilla extract

¼ cup cane sugar

1 tablespoon cinnamon

Preheat the oven to 350°F and line two large baking sheets with parchment paper.

In a small bowl, combine the flaxseed and water and set aside to thicken.

In a large bowl, stir together the all-purpose flour, oat flour, baking powder, baking soda, and salt.

In a medium bowl, place the maple syrup, coconut oil, peanut butter, vanilla, and the flaxseed mixture. Whisk until very smooth. Pour the wet ingredients into the bowl of dry ingredients and stir until well combined.

In a shallow bowl, stir together the sugar and cinnamon.

Use a 1-tablespoon cookie scoop to scoop the dough and use your hands to roll it into balls. Roll the balls in the cinnamon-sugar mixture, place them on the baking sheets, and press down to flatten slightly.

Bake for 8 to 10 minutes, or until lightly browned. Cool on the pan for 10 minutes, then transfer to a wire rack to finish cooling.

MAKES 24 TO 30 COOKIES

VEGAN

RASPBERRY BASIL BLENDER SORBET

This recipe is so simple—the trick is blending it when the frozen raspberries are *just* soft enough to blend (about 5 minutes out of the freezer) but not so soft that they defrost while blending. Use your blender baton to help the frozen raspberries disperse. This sweet, tangy sorbet is of course delicious and refreshing served on its own, but I love it next to a scoop of vanilla ice cream for a creamy contrast.

❖

4 cups frozen raspberries

1 cup maple syrup

½ cup fresh basil leaves

½ cup canned lite coconut milk

½ cup water

1 tablespoon plus 1 teaspoon fresh lemon juice

¼ teaspoon sea salt

Optional: *Push the sorbet through a sieve to remove the raspberry seeds. Freeze until set.*

Place the raspberries, maple syrup, basil, coconut milk, water, lemon juice, and salt in a high-speed blender. Blend on low and gradually work up to high speed. Blend until the mixture is very smooth and thick, like the texture of soft serve. (Don't overmix or the sorbet will start melting from the heat of the blender.)

Serve immediately as soft serve or pour into a freezer-safe container and freeze until firm but still scoopable, 2 to 3 hours. If freezing overnight, let it sit at room temperature to soften for approximately 15 minutes before serving.

SERVES 6 TO 8

VEGAN & GLUTEN-FREE

CHOCOLATE CAKE WITH SWEET POTATO FROSTING

A few years ago, I (along with the rest of the internet) fell in love with chocolate avocado frosting. It does have a downside, though—due to its avocado base, anything that you frost with it must be eaten within a day or two. That means frosting a cake with it would go against my "everything in moderation" rule. So enter the mighty sweet potato! Puree mashed sweet potato and chocolate with a bit of coconut oil, and slather it on this easy, one-bowl cake that you can enjoy in moderation. In theory.

Sweet Potato Frosting

2 large sweet potatoes

¾ cup semisweet chocolate chips

¼ cup cacao or unsweetened cocoa powder

2 tablespoons melted coconut oil

⅛ teaspoon sea salt

Chocolate Cake

1½ cups all-purpose flour

1 cup whole wheat flour

1 cup unsweetened cocoa powder

2 teaspoons baking soda

1 teaspoon sea salt

½ teaspoon cinnamon

2 cups almond milk

1½ cups maple syrup

½ cup extra-virgin olive oil

2 teaspoons apple cider vinegar

2 teaspoons vanilla extract

Make the sweet potato frosting: Preheat the oven to 425°F. Use a fork to poke a few holes into the sweet potatoes. Place on a baking sheet or on a piece of foil and roast until very tender, about 60 minutes. Let the potatoes cool slightly, then measure 1½ cups of the soft flesh. In a food processor, puree the sweet potato, chocolate chips, cocoa powder, coconut oil, and salt. The heat of the sweet potato will melt the chocolate. Chill until ready to use.

Preheat the oven to 350°F and grease two (8-inch or 9-inch) cake pans.

In a large bowl, stir together the flours, cocoa powder, baking soda, salt, and cinnamon. To the same bowl, add the almond milk, maple syrup, olive oil, apple cider vinegar, and vanilla. Stir until combined. Pour the batter into the prepared cake pans and bake for 25 to 30 minutes, or until the top of the cake springs back when pressed or a toothpick inserted in the center comes out clean.

Place the pans on cooling racks and cool for 10 minutes. Gently loosen the sides of each cake with a knife. Remove the cakes from the pans and place back on the racks to cool completely. Frost the cakes, layer, and serve. Store leftover cake in the fridge.

SERVES 12

VEGAN

CHERRY PIE CHIA PARFAITS

This recipe was originally intended as a breakfast, but as soon as I tried this combo I exclaimed, "This is dessert!" Creamy chia pudding, jammy tart cherries, and a crunchy granola topping are great as a midday snack or an after-dinner treat. Tart cherries are known to help with inflammation, so it's a dessert you can feel good about. Note that tart cherry season is short, so I almost always buy them frozen.

Chia Pudding

1 cup full-fat canned coconut milk

1 cup almond milk

¼ cup chia seeds

1 tablespoon maple syrup

¼ teaspoon cinnamon

⅛ teaspoon sea salt

Granola

1 cup gluten-free whole rolled oats

¼ cup chopped walnuts

1 teaspoon cinnamon

¼ teaspoon sea salt

1 tablespoon melted coconut oil

2 tablespoons maple syrup

1 tablespoon creamy almond butter

Parfaits

1 cup frozen tart cherries, thawed

¼ cup coconut flakes (optional)

Make the chia pudding: In a lidded 3- to 4-cup jar, combine the coconut milk, almond milk, chia seeds, maple syrup, cinnamon, and salt. Cover and shake to combine. Chill overnight.

Make the granola: Preheat the oven to 300°F and line a baking sheet with parchment paper.

In a medium bowl, combine the oats, walnuts, cinnamon, and salt. Drizzle in the coconut oil and maple syrup and add the almond butter. Stir until combined. Scoop the granola onto the baking sheet and press the mixture into a 1-inch-thick circle. This will encourage clumping. Bake for 15 minutes, rotate the pan halfway, and use a fork to gently break the granola apart just a bit. Bake for 15 minutes more, or until golden brown. Let cool for 15 minutes before serving.

Assemble the parfaits with the chilled chia pudding, granola, tart cherries, and coconut flakes on top, if desired.

SERVES 4 TO 6   VEGAN & GLUTEN-FREE

FRUIT CRUMBLES

4 WAYS

BASE CRUMBLE RECIPE

⅓ cup gluten-free whole rolled oats

⅓ cup chopped walnuts, pecans, or pistachios

¼ cup almond flour

¼ cup brown sugar or coconut sugar

½ teaspoon cinnamon

⅛ teaspoon sea salt

1 tablespoon firm coconut oil, plus more for greasing

1 scant tablespoon water

3½ cups fruit filling

Preheat the oven to 350°F and grease a 7×9-inch baking dish with coconut oil.

In a food processor, place the oats, nuts, almond flour, sugar, cinnamon, and salt and pulse until just combined. Add the coconut oil and pulse again. Add the water and pulse again.

In a medium bowl, mix together the fruit filling. Transfer to the baking dish, top with the crumble, and bake for 20 to 28 minutes, or until the fruit is soft and the topping is lightly browned.

SERVES 4 TO 6   VEGAN

Serve with vanilla ice cream!

1 PEACH & BLACKBERRY

3 peaches, pitted and sliced
1 cup blackberries
1 teaspoon vanilla extract
½ tablespoon fresh lemon juice

2 STRAWBERRY RHUBARB

2½ cups strawberries, hulled and halved
1 cup chopped rhubarb
2 teaspoons vanilla extract
1 tablespoon all-purpose flour

3 BLUEBERRY CHIA

3½ cups blueberries
1 tablespoon chia seeds
2 teaspoons vanilla extract
1 tablespoon fresh lemon juice

4 SPICED GINGER PEAR

3 ripe pears, cored and diced
2 teaspoons grated fresh ginger
½ cup dried cranberries
1 teaspoon apple cider vinegar

DATE BALLS

START WITH 10 SOFT MEDJOOL DATES + ½ TEASPOON SEA SALT.

Choose a recipe from the following page and add all the ingredients to a food processor. Pulse until the mixture sticks together when pinched. If it's too crumbly, add water, 1 teaspoon at a time. Roll the mixture into balls, then roll the balls into toppings, as listed. Enjoy as a treat! Store these at room temperature.

LEMON COCONUT

1½ cups shredded coconut
1 cup macadamia nuts
⅓ cup cashew butter
1½ tablespoons lemon zest
1 tablespoon fresh lemon juice
¼ teaspoon ground turmeric
Roll in: ⅓ cup shredded coconut +
½ teaspoon lemon zest

PB&J

1¼ cups oat flour
1 cup peanuts
⅓ cup peanut butter
3 tablespoons water
Roll in: ½ cup crushed
freeze-dried strawberries

CARROT GRANOLA

1½ cups whole rolled oats
1 cup walnuts
⅔ cup peeled and chopped carrot
⅓ cup almond butter
¼ cup dried currants
½ teaspoon cinnamon

MATCHA PISTACHIO

1½ cups almond flour
1 cup shelled pistachios
⅓ cup cashew butter
¼ teaspoon matcha powder
1 tablespoon water
Roll in: ⅓ cup crushed pistachios +
¼ teaspoon matcha powder

TAHINI SPICE

1½ cups shredded coconut
⅓ cup tahini
1 cup sesame seeds
2 tablespoons maple syrup
1 teaspoon cinnamon
¼ teaspoon ground cardamom
Roll in: ⅓ cup sesame seeds

COOKIE DOUGH

1½ cups oat flour
1 cup walnuts
⅓ cup almond butter
1 teaspoon vanilla extract
2 tablespoons water
Fold in: ½ cup chocolate chips

DRI

NKS

HOMEMADE HIBISCUS COLD BREW TEA

Jack and I are obsessive iced tea drinkers. Whereas some people thrive on coffee, we require our daily dose of antioxidant-filled tea. I've always loved the bold, pungent hibiscus tea that I order at some of my favorite lunch spots. Once I started making my own at home, I was even more hooked. For a clean taste, I like to cold-brew my hibiscus tea. You can find hibiscus flowers online—they're inexpensive, and they come in a giant bag so that you can enjoy this tea for a long time to come!

¼ cup hibiscus flowers

4 cups cold filtered water

1 small bunch mint, for garnish

¼ cup raspberries, for garnish

Sweetener of choice (optional)

Place the hibiscus flowers in a large jar or medium pitcher. Add the water, stir to combine, and chill until bright red, at least 20 minutes. For a deeper color and flavor, chill overnight. Strain, serve over ice, and sweeten to taste, if desired. Garnish with fresh mint and raspberries, as desired.

SERVES 4

VEGAN & GLUTEN-FREE

BLUSH LEMON ROSÉ COCKTAIL

I love lemons. I love rosé. I love this cocktail.

———◆◆———

¼ cup rosé wine

1 tablespoon vodka

1 tablespoon triple sec

½ tablespoon fresh lemon juice, plus lemon slices for garnish

Pour the rosé, vodka, triple sec, and lemon juice into a 4-ounce cocktail glass. Stir, and garnish with a lemon slice.

SERVES /

VEGAN & GLUTEN-FREE

LEMON FENNEL COCKTAIL

There's a lemony cocktail that I love called the Corpse Reviver because it's filled with the flavor of fennel and herbs. In this lighter version, fennel tea, fennel, and fresh basil bring the flavor that absinthe and chartreuse supply in the traditional recipe. This cocktail got me hooked on making drinks with tea—turn to page 272 for more "tea-tail" ideas!

½ cup gin

½ cup plus 2 tablespoons steeped and chilled fennel tea*

¼ cup lemon juice

2 tablespoons maple syrup

½ cup coarsely chopped fennel

8 fresh basil leaves

Handful of ice

Sparkling water, for topping

Lemon peel, for garnish

*I like Traditional Medicinals® Organic Fennel Tea.

In a cocktail shaker, combine the gin, fennel tea, lemon juice, maple syrup, fennel, basil, and ice. Shake well and pour into four 6-ounce glasses. Top with sparkling water and garnish with the lemon peel.

SERVES 4

VEGAN & GLUTEN-FREE

STRAWBERRY, PEACH & BASIL SANGRIA

This sangria is my go-to drink for summer parties. It takes just a few minutes to make, but it's sure to impress guests. This is a great recipe to mix up a few hours before serving: the flavors deepen as they mingle in the fridge.

❖

1 bottle (750 mL) pinot grigio

⅓ cup Lillet Blanc

2 peaches, pitted and sliced

1 cup strawberries, hulled and halved

1 cup loosely packed basil

Ice, for serving (optional)

Combine all ingredients in a pitcher. Stir, and chill until ready to serve. Serve over ice, if desired.

SERVES 6

VEGAN & GLUTEN-FREE

TEA-TAILS

Raise your glass to antioxidants with these refreshing cocktails made with tea! Steep and chill teas before mixing into the cocktails.

1

MINT TEA MULE

2 tablespoons vodka
¼ cup mint tea
¼ cup ginger kombucha
Handful of ice
Handful of mint

2

GINGER TEA GIMLET

¼ cup gin
¼ cup ginger tea
1 tablespoon lime juice
1 teaspoon agave nectar
Splash of sparkling water

3

PEACH TEA PALOMA

¼ cup grapefruit juice
¼ cup sparkling water
¼ cup peach black tea
¼ cup tequila
1 teaspoon agave nectar
1 tablespoon lime juice

4

ORANGE TEA OLD FASHIONED

¼ cup bourbon
1 teaspoon maple syrup
¼ cup orange tea
1 orange slice, for garnish
2 splashes bitters

*I love my cocktails lightly sweet;
add more sweetener to taste.*

5

6

7

8

GREEN TEA
TINI

¼ cup gin
¼ cup green tea
½ teaspoon agave nectar
2 olives, for garnish

MATCHA
MOJITO

¼ teaspoon matcha
¾ cup sparkling water
3 tablespoons rum
2 tablespoons lime juice
Handful mint leaves
2 handfuls ice
1 teaspoon agave nectar

HIBISCUS
HIGHBALL

¼ cup gin
½ cup hibiscus tea
1 tablespoon lime juice
1 teaspoon agave nectar
2 handfuls ice
¼ cup sparkling water

LEMON TEA
LEMONADE

Sugar plus cayenne for the rim
¼ cup vodka
¼ cup plus 2 tablespoons
lemon tea
1 tablespoon lemon juice
1 teaspoon maple syrup
Handful of crushed ice

Cocktails 1 to 4, 7, and 8: Stir together the ingredients, pour, and serve.
Cocktail 5: Shake together the ingredients, pour, and serve.
Cocktail 6: Whisk matcha and water until smooth. Stir in the remaining ingredients, pour, and serve.

HOME
EXT

MADE
RAS

FEATURED IN:

Zucchini Noodle Puttanesca (page 177)

EASY QUINOA SAGE VEGGIE BALLS

Veggie "meatballs" are fun to eat, but they can be fussy to make. I worked really hard to streamline this recipe so that the ingredient list is short and the steps are quick. Quinoa gives these protein, walnuts give them texture, and sage and chili powder give them a nice depth of flavor. But the secret ingredient that binds these balls together is hummus! Serve them with the Zucchini Noodle Puttanesca (page 177), in salads, or on grain bowls, or tuck them inside a soft ciabatta roll with big scoops of marinara sauce.

1½ cups cooked quinoa (page 22)

1 medium carrot, shredded (½ cup)

1 shallot, chopped (⅓ cup)

½ cup walnuts

2 garlic cloves

1 teaspoon chili powder

¼ cup chopped sage

1 cup chopped fresh parsley or cilantro

¼ teaspoon sea salt

⅓ cup store-bought hummus

⅔ cup panko bread crumbs

Extra-virgin olive oil, for drizzling

Preheat the oven to 400°F and line a baking sheet with parchment paper.

In a food processor, place the quinoa, carrot, shallot, walnuts, garlic, chili powder, sage, parsley, and salt. Pulse until combined, scraping down the sides of the food processor as needed. Add the hummus and pulse again. Remove the blade of the food processor and stir in the panko.

Use a 2-tablespoon scoop to form the mixture into balls. Place them on the baking sheet and drizzle lightly with olive oil. Bake for 20 to 25 minutes or until firm and lightly crisp on the outside.

MAKES 16 BALLS   **VEGAN**   **GLUTEN-FREE:** Use gluten-free panko.

QUICK PRESERVED LEMONS

I love preserved lemons, but I don't love the time that's required to preserve them. I thought there had to be a quicker way—a "quick pickled" way, perhaps—and there is! This simple recipe is based on Mark Bittman's quick preserved lemons. Since chopped lemons soften faster than whole lemons, this has become my go-to method.

---

2 thin-skinned organic Meyer lemons

1 tablespoon cane sugar

½ tablespoon sea salt

Finely dice the lemons, including the peel. Remove the seeds as you dice. Place the lemons, sugar, and salt in a lidded jar. Cover and shake. Chill for at least 3 hours, preferably overnight. The lemons will last for about 1 week.

MAKES 1½ CUPS | VEGAN | GLUTEN-FREE

LEMON SALSA VERDE

This simple condiment has such a bright pop of flavor. It livens up roasted vegetables, and it's delicious spooned onto simple pastas.

---

3 tablespoons diced Quick Preserved Lemons (above)

¼ cup finely chopped parsley or basil

2 teaspoons capers

2 tablespoons toasted pine nuts

¼ teaspoon red pepper flakes and/or 1 tiny red chile pepper, thinly sliced

Sea salt and freshly ground black pepper

2 tablespoons extra-virgin olive oil

In a medium bowl, combine the preserved lemons, parsley, capers, pine nuts, red pepper flakes, and pinches of salt and pepper. Stir in the olive oil.

MAKES ½ CUP | VEGAN | GLUTEN-FREE

HOMEMADE HARISSA

The secret to great harissa is that you have to make it yourself! It's easy to mix together, and it's a wonderful condiment to keep on hand. It'll last for a few weeks in the fridge, and you'll find yourself dolloping it on eggs and slathering it on sandwiches to instantly pep things up.

---

1 dried ancho, guajillo, or pasilla chile

1 medium red bell pepper*

½ teaspoon caraway seeds

2 garlic cloves, minced

½ teaspoon ground cumin

½ teaspoon ground coriander

Heaping ¼ teaspoon sea salt

2 tablespoons fresh lemon juice

1½ tablespoons extra-virgin olive oil

Freshly ground black pepper

¼ teaspoon red pepper flakes (optional)

½ cup sunflower seeds or pine nuts (optional)

If you choose to use a jarred roasted red bell pepper, omit the ¼ teaspoon sea salt. Season to taste.

Cut off the stem and remove the seeds from the dried chile. Pour 2 cups boiling water into a bowl, add the dried chile, and soak for 20 minutes.

Meanwhile, roast the red pepper: Char the pepper whole over a gas burner or under a broiler until the skin is blackened all over. Remove from the heat and place in an airtight container for 10 minutes. Peel and remove the loose skin. Slice off the stem and remove the membranes and seeds.

Toast the caraway seeds on the stove until fragrant, 30 seconds to 1 minute. Drain the chile.

In a food processor, place the chile, roasted red pepper, caraway seeds, garlic, cumin, coriander, salt, lemon juice, olive oil, and a few grinds of black pepper. Process until smooth, scraping down the sides of the processor as needed. Season to taste. If you prefer spicy harissa, add the red pepper flakes and pulse again.

For a thicker, spreadable consistency (especially if you're making the Charred Cauliflower Pitas on page 211), add the sunflower seeds or pine nuts to the processor and process until smooth.

MAKES 1 CUP

VEGAN | GLUTEN-FREE

FEATURED IN:

Breakfast Polenta Bowls with Chimichurri (page 49)
Chimichurri Potato Salad (page 119)

CHIMICHURRI

When you have extra herbs lying around, make chimichurri! This recipe uses fresh parsley, but cilantro works here too. Drizzle this bright sauce on any grilled or roasted vegetable.

⅓ cup extra-virgin olive oil, plus more as needed

3 tablespoons white wine vinegar

1 garlic clove, minced

½ teaspoon red pepper flakes

¼ teaspoon smoked paprika

½ teaspoon sea salt

½ cup finely chopped fresh parsley

¼ teaspoon dried oregano

In a small bowl, combine the olive oil, vinegar, garlic, red pepper flakes, smoked paprika, salt, parsley, and oregano. If your chimichurri tastes too sharp, add up to ¼ cup more olive oil.

MAKES ¾ CUP

VEGAN   GLUTEN-FREE

VEGAN RICOTTA

This is my go-to "ricotta." The crumbled tofu gives it a ricotta-like texture,
and the cashew cream makes it rich and creamy. Stuff this into shells,
layer it into lasagna, or make the lasagna soup (my personal favorite) on page 93.

4 cups medium-packed fresh spinach

2 small garlic cloves

¾ cup raw cashews

½ cup plus 2 tablespoons water

3 tablespoons fresh lemon juice

½ teaspoon sea salt, plus more to taste

Freshly ground black pepper

1 cup crumbled extra-firm tofu

1 teaspoon dried oregano

½ teaspoon lemon zest

¼ teaspoon red pepper flakes

Fill a large pot with 1 inch of water and insert a steamer basket. Place the spinach and the garlic in the basket and bring to a boil. Cover and steam for 2 minutes, or until the spinach is wilted but still bright green. Remove the garlic and set aside. Scoop the spinach onto a kitchen towel or paper towels and squeeze out the excess water. Roughly chop.

In a blender, place the garlic, cashews, water, lemon juice, salt, and a few grinds of black pepper. Process until creamy.

In a medium bowl, mix together the tofu, steamed spinach, oregano, lemon zest, red pepper flakes, and a few grinds of black pepper. Stir in the cashew cream. Taste and add more salt, if desired.

MAKES 1½ CUPS   VEGAN   GLUTEN-FREE

FEATURED IN: ===================

Zucchini Verde Vegan Enchiladas (page 157)

TOMATILLO SALSA

One of the things that I loved most about living in Austin was that there were great salsas everywhere. It gave me an appreciation for freshly made salsa because it's so much more flavorful than salsa that comes in a jar. It's easy to make too—just roast and blend.

———————◆———————

6 medium tomatillos

¼ medium yellow onion, cut into large chunks

1 jalapeño pepper, stemmed

2 garlic cloves, unpeeled, wrapped in foil

½ teaspoon lime zest

1½ tablespoons fresh lime juice

1½ tablespoons extra-virgin olive oil, plus more for drizzling

¼ cup chopped fresh cilantro

½ to ¾ teaspoon sea salt

Preheat the oven to 450°F and line a baking sheet with parchment paper.

Remove the husks and rinse the tomatillos under cool water to remove the stickiness. Place the tomatillos, onion, and jalapeño on the baking sheet, drizzle with olive oil and a generous pinch of salt, and toss. Add the wrapped garlic to the baking sheet and roast for 15 to 20 minutes, or until the tomatillos are soft and well browned.

Unwrap the garlic from the foil, peel it, and transfer to the bowl of a food processor. Add the roasted vegetables, lime zest, lime juice, olive oil, cilantro, and salt and pulse until finely chopped. Season to taste.

MAKES 1½ CUPS | VEGAN | GLUTEN-FREE

FEATURED IN:

Cozy Vegan Mushroom & White Bean Potpie (page 141)
Leek & Radish-Green Tart (page 181)

VEGAN PIE CRUST

This is a simple, versatile recipe that can be used to make sweet or savory pies. It uses coconut oil instead of butter, shortening, or lard. If you're making a savory pie, be sure to use refined coconut oil so that your pie crust doesn't have a coconut flavor.

❖

¾ cup whole wheat pastry flour

¾ cup all-purpose flour, plus more for rolling

1 tablespoon cane sugar

½ teaspoon sea salt

½ cup plus 1 tablespoon refined* coconut oil, solid but still scoopable

3 to 4 tablespoons ice water

1½ cups dried beans, as pie weights

Use refined instead of virgin or unrefined coconut oil to avoid giving the crust a coconut flavor.

In a medium bowl, whisk together the flours, sugar, and salt. Transfer half of the flour mixture to a food processor and scoop in the coconut oil by large separate spoonfuls. Pulse until the mixture starts to become crumbly, 12 to 16 pulses, then add the remaining flour and pulse until the mixture resembles coarse sand, about 8 more pulses.

Transfer the crumbly dough back to the original bowl. Add the ice water, 1 tablespoon at a time, and use a rubber spatula to fold and form the dough until it sticks together in a cohesive ball. Knead the dough a few times to get it to come together in a smooth ball. Form the dough into a 1½-inch-thick disk, wrap it in plastic wrap, and chill for 30 minutes.

Preheat the oven to 350°F. Roll out the crust to fit a 9- to 11-inch pie or tart pan. Poke holes in the crust with a fork and cover with a sheet of parchment paper. Add dry beans as pie weights and prebake for 20 minutes. Remove beans, fill with desired filling, and bake 18 to 20 minutes more, or for the time specified in the final pie or tart recipe.

SERVES 6 TO 8   VEGAN

FEATURED IN:

Pizza With Apples, Leeks & Lemon Zest Labneh (page 183)

HOMEMADE PIZZA DOUGH

This is our favorite everyday pizza dough recipe. The inspiration came from the fresh multigrain pizza dough that I like to buy at Whole Foods when I'm too lazy to make my own! This dough has a substantial, chewy crust because of some hidden quinoa mixed in, while the flaxseed adds a bit of a nutty flavor. It's easy to make—especially if you're like me and you assign your husband the task!

———————❖———————

¾ cup warm water (105 to 115°F)

1½ teaspoons maple syrup

1 (¼-ounce) package active dry yeast

1 cup white whole-wheat flour

1 cup all-purpose flour

½ cup cooked quinoa (page 22)

1 tablespoon ground flaxseed

1 teaspoon sea salt

2 tablespoons extra-virgin olive oil

In a small bowl, stir together the water, maple syrup, and the yeast. Set aside for 5 minutes, until the yeast is foamy.

In the bowl of a stand mixer fitted with a dough hook, place the flours, quinoa, flaxseed, and salt. Mix on medium speed until combined. Add the yeast mixture and 1 tablespoon of the olive oil. Mix on medium speed until the dough forms into a ball around the hook, 5 to 6 minutes. If the dough is too dry to form a ball, add water ½ tablespoon at a time until the mixture comes together. If the dough is too sticky, add a little more flour.

Turn the dough out onto a lightly floured surface and gently knead into a smooth ball.

Brush a large bowl with the remaining 1 tablespoon of olive oil and place the dough inside. Cover with plastic wrap and set aside to rise until the dough has doubled in size, about 1 hour.

Turn the dough out onto a floured surface. Stretch to fit a 14-inch pizza pan. Cover and let the stretched dough rest for 10 minutes.

Bake according to the pizza recipe you are using.

MAKES I POUND dough, enough for 1 large or 2 small pizzas   **VEGAN**

FEATURED IN:

Roasted Cauliflower Pasta with Yogurt & Harissa (page 215)
Grilled Radishes with Chickpeas & Radish-Green Goddess (page 221)

MARINATED CHICKPEAS

I use chickpeas in so many recipes throughout this book, but when I want to use them in a "no-recipe" kind of way—tossed in salads or onto grain bowls— I marinate them in this simple mixture. Whether you marinate them for 5 minutes or for a few days, their bland flavor will become bright and zippy. Play around with using different fresh herbs depending on what you have on hand.

1½ cups cooked chickpeas, drained and rinsed (page 23)

½ tablespoon extra-virgin olive oil

1 tablespoon fresh lemon juice

½ garlic clove, minced

¼ teaspoon Dijon mustard

½ teaspoon sea salt, plus more to taste

2 tablespoons chopped fresh herbs

In a medium bowl, combine the chickpeas, olive oil, lemon juice, garlic, mustard, salt, and fresh herbs. Chill until ready to use.

MAKES 1½ CUPS

VEGAN & GLUTEN-FREE

ROASTED CHICKPEAS

There are so many complicated methods for roasting chickpeas out there, but I've found that with chickpeas, and with life, simple is best. Here's my go-to ultra-straightforward method. Feel free to spice these up with pinches of smoked paprika, cayenne, chili powder, or curry powder if you like!

1½ cups cooked chickpeas, drained and rinsed (page 23)

Extra-virgin olive oil, for drizzling

Sea salt and freshly ground black pepper

Pinches of smoked paprika or chili powder (optional)

Preheat the oven to 400°F and line a baking sheet with parchment paper. Place the chickpeas on the baking sheet and toss with a drizzle of olive oil and sprinkles of salt and pepper. Roast 20 minutes, or until crispy. Remove from the oven and toss with the smoked paprika, if using.

MAKES 1½ CUPS

VEGAN & GLUTEN-FREE

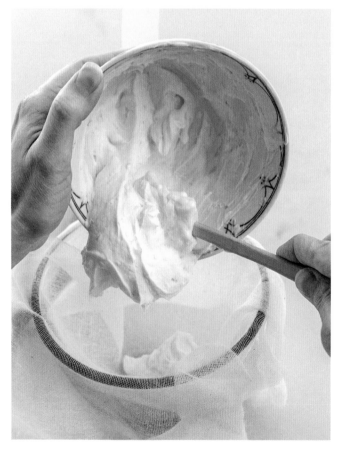

LEMON ZEST LABNEH

I don't know where labneh has been all my life, but now that I've discovered it, there's no turning back. I love how its texture is similar to goat cheese, but the flavor is less funky and more mild. To make this fresh cheese very bright, I like to stir in lemon zest.

1 cup whole milk Greek yogurt

3 teaspoons lemon zest (1 small lemon)

Heaping ¼ teaspoon sea salt

In a small bowl, mix together the yogurt, lemon zest, and salt.

Scoop the mixture onto a layer of cheesecloth. Bring the edges of the cheesecloth together, tie it around a wooden spoon, and place the spoon across the top of a medium bowl so that the labneh hangs in the center but does not touch the bottom of the bowl. Chill overnight.

Unwrap, and the labneh should be a soft yet cohesive ball where the edges are able to pull away from the cheesecloth.

Use as a cheese spread, or dollop onto salads, pizza, or flatbread.

MAKES ½ CUP

GLUTEN-FREE

FEATURED IN:

Zucchini & Radish Carpaccio Crostini (page 67)

Pizza with Apples, Leeks & Lemon Zest Labneh (page 183)

Pickles

ONE BRINE, FOUR WAYS

WHITE VINEGAR

2 cups

WATER

2 cups

CANE SUGAR

⅓ cup

+ 2 TABLESPOONS SEA SALT

Heat in a medium saucepan over medium heat. Stir until the sugar dissolves,
about 1 minute. Let cool and pour over vegetables in 2 (16-ounce) jars. Chill overnight.

Brine yields enough for 2 jars. Make two of the same type of pickle,
or mix and match vegetables and spices, using the same brine for all.

1

CUCUMBER DILL

2 small cucumbers
1 small dill sprig
2 garlic cloves, halved
1 teaspoon mustard seeds
1 teaspoon mixed peppercorns

2

YELLOW SQUASH

2 small yellow squash
1 cilantro sprig
2 garlic cloves, halved
1 teaspoon coriander seeds
1 teaspoon mixed peppercorns

3

RED ONIONS

2 small red onions, thinly sliced
2 garlic cloves, halved
1 teaspoon mixed peppercorns

4

CAULIFLOWER

1½ cups small cauliflower florets
1 small red chile pepper
1 teaspoon whole cumin seeds
1 teaspoon mixed peppercorns
¼ teaspoon ground turmeric

MARINARA SAUCE

2 tablespoons extra-virgin olive oil

⅓ cup minced shallot

2 garlic cloves, minced

¼ teaspoon sea salt, plus more to taste

Freshly ground black pepper

1 (28-ounce) can whole tomatoes

2 teaspoons balsamic vinegar

¼ teaspoon dried oregano

Pinch of red pepper flakes

¼ teaspoon cane sugar

¼ cup fresh basil, sliced

Heat the olive oil in a medium pot over low heat. Add the shallot, garlic, salt, and a few grinds of black pepper and cook for 3 minutes, stirring often.

Add the tomatoes and their juices, balsamic vinegar, oregano, and red pepper flakes. Use a potato masher to crush the tomatoes. Simmer over low heat for 20 minutes, stirring occasionally. Add the cane sugar and simmer for 10 minutes more.

Remove from the heat and stir in the fresh basil. Season to taste.

MAKES 2½ CUPS

VEGAN, GLUTEN-FREE

FEATURED IN: ═══════════

Kale and Sweet Potato Lasagna Roll-Ups (page 197)

SESAME-GINGER TAHINI

2½ tablespoons tahini

2 tablespoons fresh lemon juice

2 tablespoons maple syrup

1½ tablespoons tamari

1 tablespoon extra-virgin olive oil

1 tablespoon minced ginger

½ tablespoon sesame oil

1 garlic clove

1 tablespoon water, if needed

In a blender, place the tahini, lemon juice, maple syrup, tamari, olive oil, ginger, sesame oil, and garlic and process until smooth. If it's too thick, add the water and blend to a drizzleable consistency.

MAKES ½ to ¾ CUP

VEGAN, GLUTEN-FREE

FEATURED IN: ═══════════

Sesame-Ginger Avocado Fennel Salad (page 113)

HEALTHIER HOLLANDAISE

½ cup raw cashews

¼ cup water

2 tablespoons extra-virgin olive oil

2 teaspoons fresh lemon juice

¼ teaspoon Dijon mustard

½ garlic clove

⅛ teaspoon ground turmeric

¼ teaspoon sea salt

Freshly ground black pepper

In a high-speed blender, place the cashews, water, olive oil, lemon juice, mustard, garlic, turmeric, salt, and a few grinds of black pepper and process into a smooth sauce.

MAKES ¾ CUP

VEGAN, GLUTEN-FREE

FEATURED IN: ══════════════════

Caprese Eggs Benedict with Healthier Hollandaise (page 41)

VEGAN CAESAR

½ cup raw cashews

1 garlic clove

2 tablespoons fresh lemon juice

2 teaspoons Dijon mustard

2 teaspoons capers, drained

½ cup water

Freshly ground black pepper

In a high-speed blender, place the cashews, garlic, lemon juice, mustard, capers, water, and a few grinds of black pepper. Blend until creamy.

MAKES ¾ CUP

VEGAN, GLUTEN-FREE

FEATURED IN: ══════════════════

Grilled Romaine Vegan Caesar Wedges (page 111)

SUNNY SPINACH HERB SPREAD

½ cup raw cashews

¼ cup water, plus more as needed

2 tablespoons extra-virgin olive oil

2 teaspoons fresh lemon juice

½ garlic clove

¼ cup chopped fresh spinach

¼ cup chopped fresh cilantro

¼ teaspoon sea salt

In a high-speed blender, place the cashews, water, olive oil, lemon juice, garlic, spinach, cilantro, and salt and process until smooth.

MAKES 1 CUP

VEGAN, GLUTEN-FREE

FEATURED IN: ═══════════════

Spring-on-a-Plate Socca Flatbread (page 153)

CASHEW LIME SOUR CREAM

1 cup raw cashews

1 cup water

1 garlic clove

2 tablespoons fresh lime juice

Heaping ¼ teaspoon sea salt

In a high-speed blender, place the cashews, water, garlic, lime juice, and salt and blend until smooth. Chill until ready to use.

MAKES 1½ CUPS

VEGAN, GLUTEN-FREE

FEATURED IN: ═══════════════

Zucchini Verde Vegan Enchiladas (page 157)

CREAMY CILANTRO SAUCE

½ cup mayonnaise

½ garlic clove, minced

¼ cup chopped fresh cilantro leaves
and stems

½ teaspoon lime zest

1 teaspoon fresh lime juice

Sea salt and freshly ground black
pepper

In a small bowl, stir together the mayo,
garlic, cilantro, lime zest, and lime juice
and season with salt and pepper. Chill until
ready to use.

MAKES ½ CUP

VEGAN: Use vegan mayonnaise.
GLUTEN-FREE

FEATURED IN: ═══════════════

*Chickpea Harissa Veggie Burgers
(page 173)*

YELLOW CURRY SAUCE

1 small sweet potato

1 teaspoon whole cumin seeds

1 teaspoon coriander seeds

10 cardamom pods, seeds removed

1½ cups full-fat canned coconut milk

2 garlic cloves

1 tablespoon grated fresh ginger

½ teaspoon ground turmeric

¼ teaspoon cayenne pepper

Zest of 1 lime

½ teaspoon white wine vinegar

½ teaspoon sea salt

Preheat the oven to 425°F. Use a fork to
poke holes in the sweet potato and roast
for 60 minutes, until soft. Measure ½ cup
of the cooked soft flesh.

Toast the cumin, coriander, and cardamom
in a small dry skillet over medium heat,
until they begin to pop, 2 to 3 minutes.

In a blender, place the ½ cup sweet potato
flesh, the toasted spices, coconut milk,
garlic, ginger, turmeric, cayenne, lime zest,
vinegar, and salt. Blend until smooth.

MAKES 2 CUPS

VEGAN, GLUTEN-FREE

FEATURED IN: ═══════════════

Sunshine Sweet Potato Curry (page 193)

STEM & SCRAP TZATZIKI

½ cup whole milk Greek yogurt

1 tablespoon extra-virgin olive oil

1 garlic clove, minced

¼ teaspoon lemon zest

1½ tablespoons fresh lemon juice

¼ cup chopped carrot tops or fennel fronds

¼ cup mixed herbs with stems (mint, dill, cilantro)

2 tablespoons water

¼ teaspoon sea salt

Freshly ground black pepper

In a small bowl, mix together the yogurt, olive oil, garlic, lemon zest, lemon juice, carrot tops, herbs, water, salt, and a few grinds of black pepper.

MAKES ¾ CUP

GLUTEN-FREE

FEATURED IN: ══════════

Roasted Carrots with Carrot Top Tzatziki (page 229)

RADISH-GREEN GODDESS DIP

1 cup loose-packed radish greens

1 garlic clove

⅓ cup loose-packed basil, chopped

½ teaspoon lemon zest

1 tablespoon fresh lemon juice

½ teaspoon honey or maple syrup

Heaping ½ teaspoon sea salt

¾ cup whole milk Greek yogurt

2 tablespoons extra-virgin olive oil

Bring a small pot of water to a boil and set a bowl of ice water nearby. Drop the greens and garlic into the boiling water to blanch. Remove the greens after about 10 seconds, or until just wilted, and transfer to the ice water. Remove the garlic 1 minute later and set aside. Drain the greens, pat dry, and chop.

In a food processor, place the radish greens, garlic, basil, lemon zest, lemon juice, honey, salt, and yogurt. Pulse until well combined. Drizzle in the olive oil and pulse again. Chill until ready to use.

MAKES 1½ CUPS

GLUTEN-FREE

FEATURED IN: ══════════

Grilled Radishes with Chickpeas & Radish-Green Goddess (page 221)

CHARRED JALAPEÑO PESTO

2 jalapeño peppers

½ cup pepitas

1 garlic clove

1 cup chopped fresh cilantro

1 cup chopped fresh parsley

2 tablespoons fresh lemon juice

½ teaspoon ground cumin

¼ teaspoon sea salt

¼ cup extra-virgin olive oil, plus more
for drizzling

Freshly ground black pepper

Over an open flame, grill the jalapeños
until blackened all over. Wrap in foil for
10 minutes to steam and soften. In a small
food processor, place the pepitas and garlic
and pulse several times. Add the cilantro,
parsley, lemon juice, cumin, salt, and a few
grinds of black pepper and pulse again.
With the blade running, drizzle in the olive
oil. Unwrap the jalapeños and remove
the stem, seeds, and ribbing, keeping the
blistered skin. Add the jalapeños to the
food processor and pulse until combined.

MAKES 1½ CUPS

VEGAN, GLUTEN-FREE

FEATURED IN: ═══════════

*Spicy Black Bean & Mango Stuffed Peppers
(page 165)*

MINT PESTO

½ cup pepitas

½ cup mint leaves

½ cup parsley

½ cup thawed frozen peas

1 small garlic clove

2 tablespoons fresh lemon juice

¼ teaspoon sea salt

¼ cup extra-virgin olive oil, plus more
as desired

In a food processor, place the pepitas, mint,
parsley, peas, garlic, lemon juice, and salt
and process to a coarse puree. With the
blade running, pour in the olive oil and
process until combined.

MAKES 1 CUP

VEGAN, GLUTEN-FREE

FEATURED IN: ═══════════

Lemon Miso Spring Green Soup (page 89)

GREEK YOGURT TARTAR SAUCE

½ cup whole milk Greek yogurt

2 tablespoons mayonnaise

2 tablespoons finely minced cilantro

1 tablespoon fresh lemon juice

1 teaspoon chopped capers

½ teaspoon Dijon mustard

½ garlic clove, minced

¼ teaspoon onion powder

¼ teaspoon chili powder

¼ teaspoon sea salt

In a small bowl, stir together the yogurt, mayo, cilantro, lemon juice, capers, mustard, garlic, onion powder, chili powder, and salt.

MAKES ¾ CUP

FEATURED IN: ===================

Breaded and Baked Artichoke "Fish" Tacos (page 155)

CARROT TOP PESTO

½ cup pepitas

1 small garlic clove

¼ teaspoon sea salt

Freshly ground black pepper

2 tablespoons fresh lemon juice

1 cup carrot tops

1 cup fresh basil

¼ cup extra-virgin olive oil

In a small food processor, place the pepitas, garlic, salt, and a few grinds of pepper and pulse until combined. Add the lemon juice, carrot tops, and basil and pulse again. With the blade running, drizzle in the olive oil and process until combined.

MAKES ¾ CUP

HORSERADISH SAUCE

½ cup raw cashews

¼ cup plus 2 tablespoons water

2 tablespoons fresh lemon juice

2 tablespoons Dijon mustard

1½ tablespoons ketchup

1 tablespoon dill pickle relish

1½ teaspoons jarred horseradish

1 small garlic clove

¼ teaspoon sea salt

In a high-speed blender, place the cashews, water, lemon juice, mustard, ketchup, relish, horseradish, garlic, and salt. Blend until smooth.

MAKES ¾ CUP

FEATURED IN: ════════════

Vegetarian Portobello Reuben Sandwiches (page 169)

QUICK PICO

1 cup diced tomato (1 to 2 small tomatoes)

½ cup diced white onion

¼ cup chopped fresh cilantro

2 tablespoons fresh lime juice

1 garlic clove, minced

½ jalapeño pepper, stemmed and diced

¼ teaspoon sea salt

In a small bowl, place the tomato, onion, cilantro, lime juice, garlic, jalapeño, and salt. Toss to combine.

MAKES 1½ CUPS

VEGAN, GLUTEN-FREE

FEATURED IN: ════════════

Broccoli Rice Black Bean Burritos (page 149)

SPECIAL-OCCASION
MENUS

SPRING SOIREE

Sesame-Ginger Avocado Fennel Salad
(page 113)

Spring-on-a-Plate Socca Flatbread
(page 153)

Asparagus, Snap Pea & Chive Blossom
Pasta (page 135)

Mint Tea Mules (page 272)

BACKYARD BBQ

Chickpea Harissa Veggie Burgers
(page 173)

Sweet Corn & Blueberry Arugula Salad
(page 123)

Chimichurri Potato Salad (page 119)

Homemade Pickles (page 296)

Peach Tea Palomas (page 272)

SUNDAY BRUNCH

Strawberry Baked French Toast
(page 47)

Caprese Eggs Benedict with Healthier
Hollandaise (page 41)

Gem Salad with Creamy Dill Dressing
(page 129)

GIRLS' NIGHT

Almond Cheese with Herbes de Provence
(page 73)

Moroccan-Spiced Carrot Salad
with Lentils (page 121)

Sunshine Sweet Potato Curry (page 193)

Lemon Olive Oil Pistachio Cake
(page 243)

Ginger Tea Gimlets (page 272)

THANK YOU

To my husband, Jack, for always believing in my hopes and dreams.

To my mom, for inspiring my healthy eating habits ever since my first red pepper. Oh, and for editing recipe after recipe after recipe over the past six years.

To my uncle Phil and aunt Judy, for inspiring us to love food together.

To Liam, for being my youngest taste-tester.

To Lucia Watson, Andrea Magyar, Farin Schlussel, Casey Maloney, Ashley Tucker, Suzy Swartz, and the teams at Avery and Penguin Canada for such a joyful book-making experience.

To Alix Frank and Denise Hernandez, for supporting the Love & Lemons brand and keeping the lights on in the kitchen.

To Trina Bentley, for designing another insanely gorgeous book. It's a dream to be able to collaborate with you.

To Phoebe Moore, for helping me get this book over the finish line. . . for testing recipes like crazy, prepping food to photo perfection, and fixing my misused commas.

To Jenn Elliott Blake, for beautifying these pages, one napkin and vintage spoon at a time.

To Judy Linden, for encouraging me to create this book!

To my wonderful recipes testers, Joanna Keohane and Elizabeth Brown.

To Warren Loy, for lending an ear and giving my manuscript a read.

And most important, a HUGE thank-you to my *Love & Lemons* blog readers . . . this book is for you, and I hope you love these recipes as much as I do!!! As always, thank you for cooking alongside me and inspiring me!